Buddhi For Beginners!

The Ultimate Guide To Incorporate Buddhism Into Your Life – A Buddhism Approach For More Energy, Focus, And Inner Peace

By Dominique Francon

© Copyright 2014

All rights reserved. No portion of this book may be reproduced - mechanically, electronically, or by any other means, including photocopying- without the permission of the publisher.

Disclaimer

The information provided in this book is designed to provide helpful information on the subjects discussed. The author's books are only meant to provide the reader with the basics knowledge of the topic in question, without any warranties regarding whether the reader will, or will not, be able to incorporate and apply all the information provided. Although the writer will make his best effort share her insights, the topic in question is a complex one, and each person needs a different timeframe to fully incorporate new information. Neither this book, nor any of the author's books constitute a promise that the reader will learn anything within a certain timeframe.

Table of Contents

Introduction: Buddhism CAN Change Your Life, Did You Know That?

Chapter 1: Who the First Buddha Was & What He Taught

Chapter 2: Buddhism Is EVERYWHERE - Being Buddha Across the World

Chapter 3: Are You Listening To Me? It's Time To Free Your Mind

Chapter 4: What's All The Fuss About Meditation?

Chapter 5: Why On Earth Should I Meditate?

Chapter 6: Can Mindfulness Really Improve My Brain?

Chapter 7: Let's Cut to The Chase - How Do I Get Started?

Chapter 8: Meditation Tips to Get Started - How to Sit & How Long Each Session Should Last (With Pictures!)

Chapter 9: How Do I Build Upon A Meditation Habit? - Make It Long Term!

Chapter 10: Tying Everything Into A Glorious Know - How Meditation Will Work For You

Chapter 11: Proving You're a Buddhist When You Don't Even Know It

Chapter 12: Karma, Rebirth, Rinse, Repeat

Chapter 13: Living In The Present Moment (Hey, It's All There Is)

Conclusion: You Don't Need to Be a Buddhist To Practice Buddhism!

Preview Of "Reiki For Beginners - The Ultimate Guide To Supercharge Your Mind, Increase Your Energy & Feel Great By Unlocking the Power of Reiki"

About the Author

Dedicated to those who love going beyond their own frontiers.

Keep on pushing,

Dominique Francon

Introduction

Buddhism CAN Change Your Life, Did You Know That?

There's a common misconception that Buddhism is somehow *harder* than Christianity. Think about Christianity: it's easy, right? So, if someone alien were to ask you to describe Christianity, what would you say to them?

Would you describe the imagery of Catholicism, the relevance of the Virgin Mary and emphasis on confessions before God?

Would you talk about the evolution of Protestantism, starting with Martin Luther and how Christianity aims to guide people to be more like Jesus Christ in their actions?

Would you start even further back, all the way back to the writing of the Bible? Before or after the Old Testament? To be truly accurate you'd have to include Abraham and Isaac, and explain most of Judaism while you're at it.

Would you talk about Episcopalians? The United Church? The Westboro Baptist Church? Anglicans? Jehovah's Witnesses? Gospel choirs? The Crusades?

In other words: where do you start, and where do you end?

The fact is that all religions are extremely complex, and Buddhism is no different. Buddhism can't be boiled down into a single phrase: "It's about achieving a Zen understanding of the world, and feeling at peace"—that only begins to describe some of the complexities of a proper Buddhist lifestyle.

But that doesn't mean that Buddhism is difficult to learn. That's why I'm writing this book. I want to help you understand Buddhism from a ground-level, from a totally introductory standpoint, so you can take from it what you'd like. This book isn't meant to convert you to any religion (everyone knows that, as far as conversions go, Buddhists are probably the least likely), but it instead aims to guide you towards understanding what has been the dominant eastern religion for over 2,000 years.

Buddhism isn't alone in this respect—there's divergence with Hinduism, Taoism and Japanese Zen philosophy. They're roughly similar in the way that Judaism, Christianity and Islam are similar—which they are, actually, because they're all based on the same original stories of Abraham and Isaac, and all deify a supremely powerful being, just in different forms. (The Jewish God was later split into three—the Father, the Son and the Holy Spirit—and Muslims interpreted Him as Allah—but He's actually the same guy in every instance.)

Similarly, there are a myriad forms of Buddhism: Mahayana, Theravada, Cheontae, Zen, Nichiren, Shingon... the list goes on.

And, in fact, Buddhism shares many moral and ethical similarities with Christianity and Judaism. Pretty much every religion, at the end of the day, advocates being a good person, doing good deeds, not committing crimes and helping others. In all respects, education and wisdom is revered over all. Buddhism is much the same. Consider this quote: "Drop by drop is the water pot filled.

Likewise, the wise man, gathering it little by little, fills himself with good."

Literally any religious figure could have gotten away with saying that. But you know what? It was the original Buddha.

In order to get the most out of Buddhism and help your day-to-day life, we're not going to focus on the little differences between Buddhism sects. I'll introduce them to you in the first two chapters, along with what Buddhism teaches and what the religion is all about *in a nutshell*, because it's important to grasp the key concepts if you want to understand how to implement it in your life. Then we'll discuss what Buddhism teaches us on a practical level, dealing with subjects such as living in the present moment, the power of meditation and yoga (which are, actually, more similar than you might believe) and how the age-old concept of karma—including rebirth and how good deeds beget happiness—can help guide us through everyday life, even if we don't believe it literally.

The fact is, like all religions, it is not only difficult but extremely dangerous to follow it 100 percent. We've come to a point as a global society—with the ease of access to information that the internet has provided, and now that we can hear so many different viewpoints, philosophies and religious beliefs—that individualizing is becoming important and popular. There's a reason that every religion is seeing smaller and smaller numbers each year. Churches report lower attendance records, and most Jews identify more with the secular Woody Allen and Jerry Seinfeld than the ancient wise man Rabbi Hillel.

And more than that, we're learning that it's not a crime to dip into multiple religions. You can turn the other cheek like Jesus says, and also celebrate Passover with your Jewish friends. We've successfully convinced ourselves that, as long as we are true and decent people, which God we believe in matters less than how we live our lives.

And you know what? That's what Buddhism teaches us.

Buddhism is a *nontheistic* religion. That means Buddhists don't believe in a One Almighty God. Buddhists instead try to find inner peace, within themselves, not relying on an outside being to teach them. It is a religion based on self-importance, self-respect and, perhaps most importantly, self-discipline. That makes it easy to adopt certain Buddhist practices into our daily lives. Heck, we do it already, all the time—think of yoga, or mantras, or we repeat to ourselves, or the belief in good and bad karma, or meditation. These are all phrases and acts adopted from Buddhism, which have seeped into our everyday lives and our everyday vocabulary.

When you think of it that way, Buddhism isn't so foreign.

But wait, you might be saying. Back up a second. If there's no God, then who are all those statues of? Who's the big fat laughing guy, and the snarling big-eared one? And who was the original Buddha, if not a God?

And you know what? I'm going to answer all those questions in the upcoming chapters. There are too many questions. Questions are crucial in Buddhism—it's a good thing to ask them. Hopefully, I'll be able to answer as many as I can.

The fact is that Buddhism, as we know it today, has been around for over 2,000 years and has been the foundation of dozens of civilizations—some successful, some now extinct. Buddhist structures, statues and temples are some of the most historically enduring and spiritually meaningful monuments in the world: think of Cambodia's mighty Ankor Wat, a massive temple complex over 1,000-years-old; Borobudur, a magnificent ancient stone pyramid in central Java, Indonesia, that welcome a gorgeous sunrise every morning; the Hill Temple, nestled between vibrant green trees and overlooking the ancient city of Kyoto, Japan; Thailand's Wat Pho, with a famously luxurious-looking reclining Buddha, said to be the birthplace of Thai massage; and South Korea's colorful temples, like Guinsa and Haeinsa, filled with chanting monks and towering stone pagodas.

Buddhism is no joke. It's not a small belief, and it's historically older than our Biblical realities, dating back to the 5th and 6th century BC. There's no excuse to be ignorant of what the eastern half of the world believes, and there's no reason we can't learn from it.

So, for now, put your mind at ease. Put on some soft, meditative music. And let's get started.

Chapter 1

Who the First Buddha Was & What He Taught

There once was a man, around 2,600 years ago, who was born in northern India, in the foothills of the Himalayan mountains, which is now part of southern Nepal. His name was Siddhartha Gautama. Gautama was born into royalty as an opulent young aristocratic prince, with a life surrounded by comfort and luxury.

But Gautama had a problem: he wasn't very happy. It's the age-old story of "money can't buy you happiness," and it doesn't buy Gautama any joy at all. He finds himself confused, restless and constantly questioning of everything. He had a philosophical mind.

So, discouraged by his lifestyle, Gautama left his palace at the age of 29 in search of greater meaning in the world. This was the first time he had left home and witnessed the outside world. He saw the problems of the world for the first time: the sick, the old, the suffering. The naïve prince was eager to learn more about these real-world problems. He started going on more trips outside the palace to interact with people more people who were diseased, vain and dying. These problems depressed him immensely, and he decided to change his lifestyle completely.

He became an ascetic—one who abstains from mortal pleasures. He threw himself into a world devoid of expensive belongings and material wealth, and began begging for alms, pure charity, in the street. His goal was humility.

Eventually someone spotted and recognized him (as a prince, you'd think it wouldn't take too long) and tried to bring him back to the world of royalty. He denied this offer, too, and instead changed course: he began seeking out every great philosophical mind of his time, looking for answers to his problems of happiness.

He went to practice yogic meditation with the masters, and excelled at it to the point of being offered to succeed the masters as a permanent teacher, but Gautama denied this offer, too. He tried a different sort of yoga under a different teacher, and attained a high plateau of meditative consciousness—again, impressed with his determination, the then-master asked him to stay. But Gautama still wasn't satisfied.

He then turned to self-mortification: a deeper kind of humility. He deprived himself of all worldly luxuries, including food. Allegedly eating only a single leaf or nut per day, he nearly starved himself to death. He wanted no part of any world that would continue to offer him luxuries of any sort, including status as a "master" or "king". The very thought of hierarchy put a bad taste in his mouth.

By now he was 35-years-old, and found himself sitting beneath what has today become famous as the Bodhi Tree, now in Bodh Gaya, India, in the distant groves near the Neranjara riverbanks. He fell, nearly unconscious due to starvation, and promised himself he wouldn't wake up until he'd found enlightenment. He then fell into a deep meditative state, and found a previously unimaginable state of clear and thorough consciousness. He began thinking about the world, the universe, the nature of life.

This took 49 days, so the legend goes.

From that point on, he was known as the Buddha—or, later, once more Buddhas start popping up throughout history (and yes, there are at least 28 more; but no, we won't get into all of them in as much detail), he became known as the Supreme Buddha. "Buddha" means, simply, "Awakened One" or "Enlightened One," so the title fits.

What Did He Learn?

It's complicated, even impossible, to know exactly what he thought that night he underwent enlightenment. Certainly, at the very least, he shoved aside asceticism and self-mortification, along with self-indulgence at every level. He essentially created Buddhism as we know it today, and though what exactly that means can be vague, he does provide some helpful guides, which are known as dharma.

He wrote down his newfound doctrine based on what we know as "The Four Noble Truths", through which followers of Buddhism can reach Nirvana. Nirvana is the end goal in Buddhism: it is a state of awesome freedom, total ease of mind and mental mastery. To translate it into religious terms, it's heaven on earth. Anyone can reach a state of mental nirvana through dedication to Buddhism and following the teachings of Gautama.

To be in a state of nirvana means to ignore greed, selfishness, anger and other distracting emotions. It is, in a word, to be emotionally *above* the rest of the world. It sounds a bit haughty, but the idea is this completely carelessness about oneself, a delicate balance between being self-centered and not being egocentric. Nirvana means being altruistic and kind, understanding selflessness enough to know how small you are in the universe, and being okay with that.

According to one story, immediately after waking up from his Enlightenment, the Buddha wasn't sure if he should teach others his dharma. He wasn't sure everyone could handle it: after all, humans are afflicted by greed and ignorance all the time, which is why he had to go through this six-year meditative process to figure it out at all. Buddha told his problem to a friend, who convinced him that at least some people will grasp his meaning. Buddha agreed to have faith, and so the dharma was born into public.

What Does He Teach?

We're going to break down Buddhism really simply for you now, just because, well, this is an eBook, and we have a lot of other topics to touch on. So excuse me as I skip some of the details and sections like the Five Skandhas and Six Realms, which basically explain how to view life, and instead focus on what the Supreme Buddha wants *you* to learn.

The Four Noble Truths

There are four realities to face when you look at the world. The Four Noble Truths were what the Supreme Buddha first taught in his very first sermons to the public, so this is very Buddha-101 appropriate.

The first truth is that *there is suffering in the world*. We may know this phrase as, "Shit happens." Basically, life can be difficult—loved ones get hit by cars, our pets get cancer, we get fired, babies die in the womb, an African child just died as you read this sentence, schools get shot up; even if you avoid all of this, in the best-case scenario, you're going to die one day. Basically, there is pain, strife and difficulty. This is a truth of the world, and the first one we must face in order to achieve enlightenment: even if our own particular lives are mostly okay (i.e. none of the above apply, save for the death bit), the world is a harsh and brutal place. The First Noble Truth tells us that we must mentally face this head-on: think about it. Believe in it. Confront it.

The second truth defines this suffering: *every suffering has a cause*. There are a few causes. One is a craving for something: for respect, for power, for control, for material happiness. The other reasons we suffer are because we are trying to define ourselves as something we are not, or do not want to be; for example, if we're sad but want to be happy, we are trying to redefine ourselves in that moment. We try to unite with experiences in the way that we want to be constantly connected to the outside world, have a past, present and future life, and be successful. Or else we crave the opposite: to not feel sad when we don't want to, or to escape from painful emotions.

The Third Noble Truth is that *your suffering can end*. It is possible, in other words, to remove ourselves from our problems. We can rethink our lives, and redefine our personalities. Once we realize how loosely tied we are to our personalities, we can work on new ones. We don't need to pretend to fit in when we don't. We don't need to impress people we don't get alone with. We could be simpler than that, and focus on affirming ourselves to ourselves alone. We need to remove the cravings from the Second Noble Truth and focus on our real needs.

The fourth and final Noble Truth is *how to end the suffering*. It's a subtle wording difference from number three, but a significant one: while three tells us *that we can* end our suffering, four begins to tell us *how*. The answer is, basically, mindful meditation; in a longer answer, the path to happiness involves what's called **The Eightfold Path**.

The Eightfold Path

The Eightfold Path is crucial to every Buddhist practice, and comprises the Fourth Noble Truth in its entirety. It is the path to enlightenment, true understanding and personal happiness.

At the risk of turning this chapter into an extremely dense introduction, I'm going to go over the Eightfold Path very quickly, in point-form, so as to not overload you all at once.

The Noble Eightfold Path is divided into eight ways to act correctly. They're called the Rights. So remember that when you read Right here, it means Right as in Objectively Correct.

The eight Rights are divided into three sub-sections, including Wisdom, Ethical Conduct and Concentration.

The two filed under *Wisdom* describe a proper Buddhist mental state:

1. **Right View** – Sometimes called "Right Perspective" or "Right Outlook", this can be summed up as the proper way of looking at the nature of things, the way the world exists in its natural form, which can adopt an almost scientific perspective: physics, chemistry and biology all dictate our world.

2. **Right Thought** – Thinking good thoughts will give you a good life. To achieve this you must mentally renounce material goods and think instead about what matters: good deeds, peacekeeping, charity and being kind towards others.

The three steps under *Ethical Conduct* progress this lifestyle into reality:

3. **Right Speech** – So, you've got those good thoughts in your head? Speak them. No lying, no wasteful chitchat, no insults.

4. **Right Action** – Talk is cheap—do good deeds. Don't kill, steal or rape.

5. **Right Livelihood** – Don't make your job an evil one. Don't create weapons, don't trade slaves, don't sell drugs, don't kill people. According to Buddha, the "business of meat" is also a no-no; sorry, butchers.

The last three, under *Concentration*, might be the hardest to achieve:

6. **Right Effort** – This describes preventative measures. If you're leading a true Buddhist life, you will need effort to actively subdue your material and worldly urges. Be mindful of the good that has no yet risen within yourself, and abstain from the evil.

7. **Right Mindfulness** – Also translated as "Right Memory", to be mindful of something means you're keeping it in mind. You should be constantly aware of every part of your body, in tune with your health and mental state, to continue your other Right ways.

8. **Right Concentration** – Also known as "Right Meditation", this simply defines an ideal meditative state: one aloof from the world, purely tranquil and absorbed by your mental cleanness.

Phew! That about sums it up. Thanks for hanging in there. I know this stuff can get a little dense at times, but, as the Noble Eightfold Path shows, it's actually pretty natural. It's the same basic morality as suggested by Abrahamic religions: think good thoughts, do good deeds, and stay that way.

The big departures in Buddhism come in the specific logic of the religion. The description of the mind and body is different from the Christian conception of the soul. Nirvana is different from heaven. But only in logical terms.

If looked at abstractly, from a bit far away, you'll find that the first of the Four Noble Truths—that there is suffering in the world—is an issue debated and tackled by every major religion in the world. Others might simply chalk it up to the old phrase, "God works in mysterious ways." The big change in Buddhism is that it tries to define that problem and, instead of promoting belief in God or Jesus to save you from such dangers and bring you to heaven, the Supreme Buddha suggests believing in yourself and overcoming these worldly problems while you're still on Earth.

This is by no means a comprehensive analysis—we still haven't gotten to karma, rebirth or the thousands of other little details that create Buddhism. But we'll get there soon.

For now, and in the next chapter, we're going to look at a few variations of Buddhism, and how it's affected the world as we know it.

Chapter 2

Buddhism Is EVERYWHERE - Being Buddha Across the World

Think about this: has any significant group been truly *satisfied* by religion? Martin Luther started Protestantism, which bore Anglicanism, because he didn't agree with the Catholic Church. There are hundreds of sects of Jews and Muslims.

It makes sense, then, that there isn't simply "one type" of Buddhist.

It's kind of ironic, when you think about it. The Supreme Buddha's main goal was to enlighten people, so they could live in harmony. Do you know what happened instead? They bickered. The argued over interpretations and over the "right way" to study the Supreme Buddha. They disagreed, and because they disagreed they created schisms in their own lives and branched off into a thousand little sects. Despite what originally Gautama wanted, his instincts were right: people don't listen.

There are two main divisions of Buddhism: Theravada and Mahayana. There are subdivisions even within those, and fringe sects beyond them, but we'll start with these two, because they're philosophically and geopolitically different.

There's a clean north-south axis that divide these two sects. We'll start with Theravada Buddhism, which is still prominent today in

India, Sri Lanka, and the Southeast Asian countries of Thailand, Cambodia, Myanmar and Laos.

Theravada Buddhism is the "original" Buddhism, and the oldest surviving of the original sects. It relies heavily on the "Pali Canon", a series of writings in the ancient Pali language and the oldest reliable source of Gautama's original teachings.

The Supreme Buddha never pretended to be a God. He actually dismissed the idea of there being a God at all—while Buddhism necessarily acknowledges and allows for the belief in other religions and deities, his teachings hinge on self-reliance and the kind of "manifest destiny" mentality that should appeal to American Conservatives. So nobody was surprised when Gautama died at 80-years-old after eating a poisonous wild mushroom. He'd had a good life.

A century or two after his death, however, memories of the Supreme Buddha became foggy, and the monastic community became politically divided over who was in charge. There were enlightened monks, called Arahats, who were basically running things and who had studied under Buddha or his direct disciples, but the majority of followers—common, everyday people—began to resent the Arahats' leadership and interpreted it as selfishly geared.

Slowly, Arahats began to grow backwards in importance, being less and less relevant to achieving enlightenment. Instead, the commoner majority began to believe in the concept of the Bodhisattva: a normal person, not enlightened, but who is trained to become a Buddha, an enlightened one. Arahats were not

Buddhas—it's like the difference between a theological professor and an actual priest. Arahats were considered more intellectuals, but lacked the "divine" power of enlightenment. There had yet never been a Buddha other than Gautama, and he was long dead.

That offshoot evolved into **Mahayana Buddhism**. The Mahayana sect, for reasons too millennium-spanning to clarify, migrated north; this is today the dominant Buddhist religion in East Asia, in countries such as South Korea, China, Japan, Mongolia and Taiwan. These Mahayana Buddhists kept most of the original Buddha's teachings, but added the possibility that anyone—no matter how common—can achieve the status of Bodhisattva, an enlightened Buddha.

That's why, when you see a fat-bellied Buddha whose stomach you should rub for good luck, he's nowhere to be found in Southeast Asian temples, which only create statues of the original Supreme Buddha, who's in general a slimmer, more gently smiling man. The fat-bellied fella is named Budai, and achieved enlightenment as a Buddha around the 10th century in China. (Fun fact: the reason you rub his belly for good luck is because the stomach, to Buddhists, is the spiritually core of a person's body; Buddhists don't believe in "souls" per se, but they also believe in every part of the body attaching a spiritual significance; the head is the most sacred point, which is why it's impolite in most Asian cultures to pat someone on the head, and the feet are the lowest and most impure part of a body, which is why you should never show your soles off to a Buddha statue.)

So while Theravada Buddhists believe in only 28 Buddhas—which in itself is a long story of Buddhist lineage, of which Gautama was the final and only Supreme Buddha—Mahayana Buddhists believe that anyone can, and has, become a Buddha. There is an infinite, countless number of Buddhas out there, including some still around today.

In other words, yes, it is entirely possible for you to become a Buddha. Statue not guaranteed.

Still later, after Mahayana Buddhism settled, more offshoots began, including **Zen Buddhism** in Japan and Korea. Zen Buddhism is unique—if you've ever been to China, Japan or South Korea, you'll have noticed a difference in temple variety to that of Southeast Asian architecture. You might also have noticed a lack of giant Buddha statues. Zen Buddhism originated in China in the 6th century, and involves a more basic approach to Buddhist meditation. It emphasizes direct insight into Buddhist teachings, and the ability to reach enlightenment through meditation and calmness. To an extent, it disregards the necessity to repeat and memorize sutras and doctrines and focuses on the basics of Buddhism: self-discipline and isolation. It caught on in Japan most prominently, and now when we think of "Zen" we think of Japanese gardens of stone and raked sand.

And then there's **Tibetan Buddhism**, which is strong in modern-day Tibet. This sect of Buddhism is also sometimes known as Tantric Buddhism. If you've heard of the Dalai Lama, that's Tibetan Buddhism: the current Dalai Lama is the 14th, and he has publicly discussed whether or not he will reincarnate into a 15th being. Tibetan Buddhism has gotten into a sticky situation with the current partially communist Chinese government, which has actually banned reincarnation from being a legal process of choosing a successor. You can read up on that one yourself.

There are a few other varieties of Buddhism, of course, like **Nichiren Buddhism**, developed by an old Japanese monk by the same name who emphasized following Gautama's Lotus Sutra, which stresses personal enlightenment; and **Pure Land**, which requires followers to purify their minds by chanting "Amitabha", the name of a particular Buddha, to help reach enlightenment, and focus on our own personal qualities.

Some of these forms might sound difficult to buy into, but they're not so obscure. Consider how ridiculous any religion or belief system sounds when heard for the first time. The story of the first Supreme Buddha isn't that far off from King David or Jesus Christ. Every culture has its heroes, and every hero has been studied and mythologized into something great, idealistic and pure for the rest of us to strive towards.

In the end, all any of these religions aim to do is give us hope. The main difference with Buddhism is that aims to teach us to find hope from within ourselves, rather than seeking outside advice or saviors. It tells us that only we can help ourselves. It's existentialist in that way, and shockingly modern.

If you learn only one thing from this book, let it be that: that an Indian man 2,600 years ago came up with the answers to existential problems long before the existentialists even asked them. He knew it was every man for himself, and that you should accept that and be happy.

Gautama never wanted to be deified like a God, and that didn't happen. But people still idolize him—literally, turned him into an idol statue, along with dozens of other famous Buddhas. It's important to remember that these are not Buddhist *gods*, because gods don't exist in Buddhism. (Although some Chinese, Korean and Japanese folklore does blend into Buddhism, and you might see ancient mystical Chinese temples with dragon gods—the ways in which history has intertwined these beliefs is amazing and baffling.)

Rather than gods, these Buddhas are considered heroes. People praying at Buddhist temples aren't praying for a Buddha to help them, but rather *asking for advice*. They look to the strength, discipline and intelligence of past Buddhist masters, and hope to replicate it, to find the same nugget of spiritual truth that they once did.

In truth, Buddhism isn't really a religion. It's more of a belief. And more than that, it's a belief in oneself.

Once you understand that, you can progress on your own path to self-fulfillment and self-empowerment. Just like the Big Buddha himself.

Chapter 3

Are You Listening To Me? It's Time To Free Your Mind

You all know the picture: a man with a shaved head and a robe, sitting cross-legged on the ground. His hands are upturned and his middle finger is gently touching his thumb, while the six other digits curve slightly outward. His eyes are closed, and he's humming softly to himself: "Ohm..."

That's meditation, right?

Well, not necessarily.

Meditation can come in all volumes and types. It's essential to the Buddhist experience, and is practiced commonly by people who don't identify as Buddhists. While there is such a thing as a strict definition of meditation, most people have adopted the word "meditation" to refer to all sorts of activities that aim to sooth the mind. Simply relaxing at home with a glass of wine by yourself and listening to classical music could be called "meditative". Some people consider turning off their brain in any respect to be meditative—including playing Tetris.

But according to Buddhism, meditation is more serious than that. To meditate is to be consciously aware of how your mind is working. You have to tune into every nook and cranny in your brain—when you make an association from one idea to another, you have to follow your natural train of thought.

This all might sound a bit vague, or like psychology but without the science. You wouldn't be wrong—but to understand the Buddhist concept of meditation, you need an open mind.

(Pun definitely intended.)

Meditation is important because meditating means we're growing our minds. Regardless of how good we try to do on our own, assuming we can't change our innate wants and desires, actual change will seem impossible. It's all too easy to assume that we can change from jealous to accepting in a matter of days. You may convince yourself that you're on the path to erasing your jealousy, but you know what? Test yourself, look up people who have the jobs you want, the money you need or the lives you wish you had, and we'll see if you've really risen above petty emotions yet.

Meditation helps us trace and control those emotions. It trains humans to develop their concepts of self-awareness—to know what's going on, so they're not slaves to their emotions. It allows us to shift gears and take control of our minds.

So, what type of meditation will be right for you?

Only you can answer that question. It requires a bit of experimentation. The Supreme Buddha Gautama devised several different approaches that had several different meanings and uses. There isn't a one-size-fits-all approach, which is why the usual stereotype of humming and sitting cross-legged isn't 100 percent accurate.

The two most common types of traditional meditation are Mindfulness of Breathing and Loving Kindness Meditation.

What is Mindfulness of Breathing?

To practice this style of meditation, you'll need to adhere to what some call the "Four Ps"—that is, place, posture, practice and problems.

First, the place. You'll need to find a quiet spot. Assuming you can't find a secluded temple nestled in a valley between the Himalayan mountains, your living room on a quiet night will have to suffice. Or use your bedroom and close the door. It's important that you not be interrupted on this mindful journey.

Second, the posture. Sit in a comfortable position—some monks are strict about not moving at all, which includes sloping down from an upright sit to a slouch. So try to avoid that. Crossing your legs while sitting on a pillow is typically regarded as the most comfortable stance. Try to keep your back straight and your hands rested on your lap. Your eyes should be closed, of course.

Third up, you've got to practice. The meditation is called "mindfulness of breathing"—so guess what? Yep, you'll have to be mindful of your breathing. That means noting every single breath taken in and exhaled out. Pay very close attention to the flow of air through your body, in and out. In and out. In and out. This requires the utmost patience—if you find yourself getting impatient with this, don't be surprised. It's only natural that sitting and listening to the sound of your own breath might sound like a waste of time.

Which is why, lastly, you'll have to confront the myriad problems that come with meditation. When you're meditating, you might feel uncomfortable in places. Your scalp might start to itch. You might become suddenly aware of how awkward it is to sit upright. The trick? These are *worldly* issues, *material* issues. These are mere problems with our bodies—the idea is that the strength of our minds can overcome them. Just keep focusing on breathing. According to the Supreme Buddha, we must "be vigilant; guard your mind against negative thoughts."

Soon that will become tricky, too. You might get distracted thinking about something else. Or you might get sleepy and actually find yourself dozing off. Try to stay alert—alert and aware of your own bodily functions, thinking circularly about breathing. Focus on breathing *exclusively*. It will feel odd the first few times, but that's the point. That's how you become profoundly calm and achieve inner peace: first for just a few moments, but soon for longer and longer periods of time.

The first time you meditate mindfully, try it out for just 10 minutes or so. Then up the ante with each subsequent session: add a minute or two (keep a stopwatch or alarm to keep track) until you're up to the standard time for people, which is around 40-45 minutes. Ideally you're doing this every day... but people are busy, so every other day, or at least two or three times a week should suffice.

What is Loving Kindness Meditation?

Mindfulness of Breathing should be the first type of meditation you try, because it's the most basic. Loving Kindness is a slightly more advanced technique.

First, it involves the same basics as Mindfulness of Breathing: sit in a comfortable position, often with your hands set on your lap, and close your eyes. Only this time, instead of focusing on breathing, you want to focus your energies and mindfulness on a mantra directed at actual people you know.

Loving Kindness is like a mantra. A mantra is an expression we say to ourselves several times a day to instill a feeling of empowerment within ourselves. For example, you might look yourself in the mirror and say, "I am strong. I am lucky. I am happy." You might repeat this mantra several times a day until you actually start believing it.

Loving Kindness Meditation requires you say a riff on the following phrase:

> "May I be happy. May I be calm. May I be safe from harm. May my mind be peaceful. May I be free to love. May I be free."

...Or something like that, anyway. There are a few variations online, so you can choose your own exact wording. But the idea is that you focus on yourself—really hunker down and think about your own personality, your own traits and wish these positive thoughts unto yourself. The trick here is to not just speak the words, but also to justify them—to think about *why* you're saying them and why you deserve the praise. If you cannot open yourself up to love, then you will be incapable of giving love when the time calls for it. You need to sincerely open yourself up to the concept of washing yourself over with this pure sense of emotion.

It might sound a bit wishy-washy, but it truly does work. Much like a bonfire that needs oxygen to flame on, you need to fuel your own meditative self with loving kindness.

Once you're finished with yourself, then you think about various people in your life and speak this mantra to them. There's a specific order to this, though. You should start with a beloved person, like your mother, father, spouse or sibling. You can sort them in your mind as a specific person (e.g. your mother) or a group of people (e.g. your family). You'll need to vary up the wording of this one so it applies to them:

> *"May my family be happy. May my family be calm. May my family be safe from harm. May my family mind be peaceful. May my family be free to love. May my family be free."*

And so on. Remember: we can only genuinely give love to others if we've already accepted it ourselves. It would be a tad hypocritical to say, "Oh, sure, I want to wish love to my girlfriend—but me? Nah, this isn't for me."

After each round of repetitions, you'll want to focus back on your body as your primary source of being in the world. Try to relax any tight muscles. If you start to get distracted thinking of something else, refocus your mind and begin repeating your Loving Kindness mantras back onto yourself.

After that, you'll want to repeat the same mantra, but for an acquaintance, someone you're not too familiar with but know in passing—perhaps a coworker, a shopkeeper, your usual bank teller or your doctor. The idea is to unify you with people you feel no emotional connection, to impose upon your worldview the fact that we are all part of a singular universe. In that light, the next mantra goes out to complete strangers—some of the seven billion people out there whom you've never met, and whom you very likely never will.

Finally, you'll have to repeat the mantra to people you downright hate. The goal should be obvious: a proper Buddhist mindset has no room for anger or hatred. Much like the teaching of Jesus Christ, the Supreme Buddha teaches us that there is no excuse for hatred or bias in the world. Ill will never helps anyone. In order to reach enlightenment, you'll have to let go of vile emotions as they sprout up, or else contort them into a way of understanding the strength of good will. If you're doing it correctly and honestly, you'll find a level within yourself that allows for acceptance, forgiveness and positivity towards others.

This Is Starting to Sound Dumb...

Okay, fair enough! Skepticism is all too common when it comes to the power of meditation, especially when the meditative powers sound like morals coming out of a Teletubbies episode. But it isn't B.S., honestly.

What we don't appreciate all too often is the power of our minds. We turn our brains off with television and video games; we justify this off-position with attention to the aesthetic world, by absorbing ourselves in fine art and film, even though we rarely take to heart the morals these films preach. (If they're decent at all.) When we're not distracting ourselves with entertainment, we're busy flickering away our thumbs on our smartphone Facebook Messenger or Twitter app, distracting ourselves with inane social politics, or even just putting too much emphasis on good grades and making enough money. We let these things infest and take over what seems important in our lives. We crave love to quell loneliness; we crave money to stave off hunger; we yearn for independence when we feel disrespected.

As the Supreme Buddha once said, "The root of suffering is attachment."

Our minds are powerful tools. If we studied meditation in school, our social priorities would be a heck of a lot different. If we can learn to extend our mental energy towards ourselves and others, we can find tangible benefits in unseen realities.

Or, at the very least, we'll start to feel better about ourselves.

Can Meditation Be Dangerous?

This is a tricky question. On the one hand, we'd assume the answer is simply "no"; meditation is only useful, and helpful in transforming us from material beings into mindfully sentient ones.

But meditation could be harmful, just as anything can be. This is especially true of people with mental disorders. Sometimes keeping to yourself alone in a room is the worst kind of torture: some people, especially those who suffer from crippling loneliness or clinical depression, might well find the idea of sitting alone thinking about themselves an impossible task. They might focus on their troubles instead of their goals. They might not believe the Loving Kindness Meditation mantras. At best, they'll waste their time; at worst, they'll grow suicidal.

Obviously, in this instance you should seek the help of a professional therapist instead of meditating alone. The interesting irony is that many professional psychiatrists and therapists actually do recommend meditation as a form of mental relaxation. It's more commonly prescribed to people who suffer from high stress, a lack of relaxation, or who are uncontrollable afraid of something. Meditation helps raise self-awareness, which can be a very healthy thing.

The other way to handle not being alone is to meditate with a group. In East Asia, monks rise every morning at around 3 a.m. and begin hiking and meditating together for hours until breakfast is served, usually at around 6. There is also no shortage of meditation teachers out there, happy to help new students master their own minds. A teacher may also help you reach new techniques—techniques far beyond the scope of this simple eBook.

With these ideas in mind, I hope you have a better grasp of meditation than you did before. In the next chapter, we're going to examine the ways in which Buddhist philosophy can help you, even if you haven't yet bought into most of what's been mentioned so far—simple ideas like karma and reincarnation that might change your approach to life.

Chapter 4

What's All The Fuss About Meditation?

Meditation has been around, some say, since antiquity. Even in prehistoric times it's been said that civilizations had performed rhythmic and repetitive chants to appease the Gods and their minds. Numerous recorded instances of meditation were discovered among artifacts related to the ancient Hindus, Buddhists, and also in Taoist China. The term meditation is actually a broad term, and can be used to describe many forms of mental or religious discipline, or a combination of both. Whatever one perceives meditation to be, in general it's a state of concentrated attention on a thought or awareness. It's a way of transforming the mind, body, and spirit.

So, since there are so many types of meditation, how do you choose which one is right for you? That could depend on several factors, including your religion, your goals, and how much spiritual awareness you're seeking to achieve. Having that said, keep in mind that meditation doesn't have to be religious -actually, it's just a tool to achieve a higher state of mind. Choose what's right for you based on what it is you wish to get out of your meditations.

Generally speaking, there are five types of meditation: mindfulness meditation, spiritual meditation, focused meditation, movement meditation, and mantra meditation.

Mindful meditation is probably the most well-known type of meditation. When meditation comes to mind, it's most likely the mindful type you're thinking of. Mindful meditation involves being aware of the sounds and activities around you. It's about letting your mind be fluid and allowing one thought to flow into the next one. With this instance of meditation, you're not really focusing on one particular thing; instead you let your mind be aware of the outside noises around you while still focusing on the thoughts flowing in and out of your head.

Spiritual meditation leans itself to the more religious crowd. This type of meditation is good for those who practice regular prayer and use it as another way of communicating with God. It requires a calm and quiet mental concentration so that you can focus on the questions or concerns at hand and address them. Spiritual meditation gives the person a relaxing and rewarding way to express their spirituality.

Focused meditation revolves around the practice of completely clearing your mind of all outside stresses and focusing on a specific thought, sound, mantra or object. By doing this, your mind stays committed to only one thought, and you'll find yourself relaxed and rejuvenated afterwards. Focused meditation allows one to stay present in the moment and circumvent the constant stream of consciousness that is always flowing through the mind.

Movement meditation involves incorporating the flow of movement into your thoughts rather than focusing on a sound, thought, or object, you focus your attention on movement. Whether it is the rise and fall of your chest as you breathe, swaying side to side or forward and back, or even something more intensive like moving your entire upper body in a rhythmical circular motion, it's all about flowing with your mind and body as one movement.

Mantra meditation deals with incorporating sound into your meditation. The sound, or mantra, is repeated throughout the session as a way of becoming one with the sound and the mind. Mantras can be said aloud or internally. Since sound exists everywhere in the universe, from the flow of a peaceful river, to your melodic breathing in and out, all of it is a mantra. By repeating a mantra during meditation, the flows of sound and your consciousness intertwine and will relax and refresh you.

The goal of meditation is to obtain a more relaxed and stress free state from where you were when you initiated the session. It's taking yourself inside your mental awareness and focusing on channeling and concentrating on thoughts that will calm your mind. It's a way of silencing the distractive thoughts by narrowing down your mind's focus so that everything else is blocked out. This results in the release of your stresses or maintaining a stronger spiritual relationship with yourself, if you are meditation for religious reasons.

Your best bet when choosing which form of meditation is right for you is to find out which one will suit your needs best. Let me take the edge off: it doesn't matter what type you choose, as long as you are comfortable with it! The benefits that will derive from each one are absolutely the same. So no worries there!

Once you find a technique that works well for you, stick with it. It may take some mental discipline and training, but once you've mastered getting your mind into that passive and aware mode needed for meditation, you'll find that the benefits will be a soothing welcome. It's important to be patient with meditation. Let go of the wanting, which means, don't go in expecting to instantly find all of the answers immediately and then get frustrated and quit because it didn't work. Keep in mind that there is no destination to reach. Your mind is an open book. Going into a meditation with no expectations will tend to work better for you.

Above all, never lose sight of the main goal: meditation is all about relaxing and enjoying. It's relaxing for the mind, body and spirit. Even relaxing before a meditation session is great for the peace of mind you'll achieve during your sessions. Whether it's taking a hot bath or listening to some whimsical music beforehand, allow yourself to know what relaxation feels like. It's important to stick with it once you start. You may get frustrated if your mind strays from time to time, but it's normal for that to happen. Think of meditation as a vacation for your mind. Just like we need a physical vacation for relaxation, our minds also need a vacation, a mental one. And with the power of meditation, your rested mind will be sharper, more relaxed, and ready to take on whatever comes next.

Chapter 5

Why On Earth Should I Meditate?

So now that you've learned a little bit about meditation and what it entails, perhaps you're wondering how it would benefit you if you were to try it. Aside from the more obvious benefits of relaxing the body and mind, meditation is proven to improve several aspects of one's health. Not only is it good for your physical and mental well-being, but it's an effective way to improve your brain function and alleviate some of the outside afflictions we face in everyday life. Meditation's health benefits include reducing stress, helping with anxiety, improving the immune system, getting a handle on addiction, sharpening the mind with more focus, helping with sleep problems, and curbing ongoing depression. Believe me, after learning about each benefit, your question is sure to go from why should I meditate, to **why shouldn't I meditate**?

Stress can be blamed for a myriad of health problems, and rightfully so. Who in this day and age isn't stressed out by day to day things? Stress wreaks havoc on the body by stopping its normal functioning. The body sees stress as an intruder and assumes there is a physical threat. Because of this, it channels its energy on that imminent threat and all other functions such as digestion and immune function tend to take a back seat. If we are constantly stressed, then our bodies are continually battling with those stressors instead of focusing on our vital internal functions. Stress activates the "fight or flight" reaction in our nervous system. Meditation helps counteract that by putting the body in more of a "rest and relax" mode. The heart rate slows down, blood pressure drops, and breathing becomes more relaxed. This relaxation response brought on by meditation can be vitally restorative to the brain and entire body, thus improving your health as well as lowering your stress levels.

While the majority of us are anxious by nature, prolonged anxiety can have many negative effects on the body. It's almost as though we're constantly looking for something to feel anxious about because we were wired to look out for the negative things that might harm us. Through meditation, however, when one is in a more mindful state of mind, anxiety has been seen to go significantly down. Researchers believe that this is because when we learn mindfulness, we are also learning how to dispel the stressors and negativity associated with our anxiety.

Although we may not be acutely aware of it, chronic stress and anxiety can wreak havoc on our immune systems. A healthy immune system is an integral part of our physical and mental health. Within the first few minutes of being stressed, our immune systems actually strengthen, sensing an attack of sorts. That's not necessarily a bad thing though. It means our body is doing its job in response to a potential physical threat. But if that stress or anxiety becomes more chronic, our immune system is constantly in a battle trying to win an impossible fight. There's been quite a bit of research done on the effects of meditation on stress levels in our bodies. And when the stress levels go down, our immune systems are able to function properly and more effectively. Meditation and the mindfulness that comes from it will not only help strengthen your immune system, but will give you a stronger resilience both mentally and physically.

When facing an addiction, be it to drugs, alcohol, or even food, when our bodies crave it, we're more than likely to obey and continue to feed that addiction. But through the mindfulness that comes with meditation, it's possible to alleviate those cravings that lead to the addiction. Since the stress levels are also being brought down, that in turn leads to the mind not wanting to turn to that crutch one leans on to help reduce the stress, such as a cigarette or a beer. Instead of constantly wanting whatever our addiction of choice is, the mind becomes more aware that it's a craving and can then adjust accordingly, making those cravings dissipate over time. The mind is indeed a powerful thing, and through meditation, you'll be able to put it to good use by finding that inner mental strength to lead a healthier lifestyle.

Between all of that stress and anxiety, who has time to sleep? Sleep problems are definitely far more common that one would think. Whether you're lying awake thinking about being prepared for tomorrow's business meeting, or you're stressing about how to pay the bills, we've all been there. Lack of sleep not only affects your performance during waking hours, but in the long run, it can affect your overall health as well. Studies have linked inadequate sleep to afflictions such as high blood pressure and obesity, among other things. One trick to using meditation to help alleviate insomnia is to be mindful that you're having trouble sleeping in the first place. By learning practical, everyday mindfulness techniques, you'll be able to get a good night's rest and tame that overactive mind that keeps you awake at night.

Over 350 million people worldwide are affected by depression in one way or another, making it one of the most prevalent mental illnesses. Depression can affect all aspects of one's life, including sleep, eating habits, relationships, and work, not to mention taking a toll on mental and physical health. The symptoms of depression can range in depth and severity, but by incorporating meditation practices into your lifestyle, you'll be able to alleviate those symptoms of depression that hold you down. By using the mindfulness techniques in meditation, the mind is more aware and able to relax those depressive thoughts.

Yet meditation's benefits aren't limited to the scope of fighting anxiety, stress, and depression. It goes way beyond. With meditation you'll be able to improve your focus extensively, which will benefit you in all facets of life -from business, to social relationships, to your daily routine. Learning how to focus one's minds is vitally important. If we are more prone to distractions, it can have an impact on our everyday lives. If we are able to resist those distractions, we will have the ability to resist impulses that may be bad for us and achieve our more long-term goals. Since meditation requires a great sense of focus, think of it as practice for carrying that focus over into your active life. The mindfulness needed for meditation already takes your mind's ability to focus on a state of mind, object, or whatever else you are meditating on in that moment. By being able to obtain that measure of focus through meditation, you'll be enhancing your ability to apply that focus and master having a more focused lifestyle.

With all of the amazing benefits meditation has to offer, there's no doubt that it's definitely worth giving it a try. Whether you're suffering from maybe only one of the mentioned afflictions, or perhaps are looking to improve your focus extensively to make a big impact in your life, by being able to tap into your mindfulness, you'll see yourself improving over time. Who knows, you may even find yourself asking...**why didn't I start meditating sooner?**

Chapter 6

Can Mindfulness Really Improve My Brain?

So there's no question that meditation can have endless positive benefits to your physical health and well-being. But can it really make a difference with your brain function? Does the power of thought and relaxation really have that much of an impact on how your brain works? Well, it's long been a saying that it really is mind over matter. But how does that really work? What is going on in our brains that allows us to tap into that mindfulness and change the way we think, function, and feel? Well, there are many factors that play a part in how meditation affects our brain function. From actual changes in brain activity, to more subtle changes like relieving stress and anxiety, the benefits can be long lasting and important for a positive change in your life.

A study done by Dr. Herbert Benson, who founded the Mind-Body Medical Institute, suggests that meditation induces physical and biochemical changes in the body. Known as the "relaxation response," these changes include a positive change in blood pressure, heart rate, metabolism, respiration, and brain chemistry. Because the nervous system is composed of a parasympathetic system, meaning an involuntary system that serves to slow the heart rate, relax sphincter muscles, and increase intestinal and glandular activity, the effects of meditation helps relax these functions, thus putting less strain on your nervous system as a whole. And when the nervous system is calmer, the entire body as a whole is more calm and relaxed.

Scientists have developed more of an understanding through using modern technology like fMRI scans as to how the brain is affected during meditation. And the results have led to more knowledge of the correlation between the mindfulness and relaxation techniques and the way the brain processes information significantly slows. This slowing is not a detrimental thing as one may perceive. We may think of a slower brain as meaning we aren't able to think or focus. On the contrary, studies have found that because of the way the brain waves are slowed during meditation, it makes one more able to focus, relax, and let the mind take a rest.

Knowing how your brain works is always a fascinating topic. But knowing what happens to it when one is meditating proves to be even more interesting. First of all, the frontal lobe, which is responsible for self-conscious awareness, reasoning, planning, and emotions, seems to go offline during meditation. Because of this, that could account for the feeling of everyday stresses escaping from your mind and body. The parietal lobe of your brain, which processes all of the sensory information around you and essentially orients you in regards to time and space, slows down its activity. This tends to strengthen the theory that while meditating, you're able to focus on one thing, thus allowing your senses to relax. The thalamus is responsible for focusing your attention on things at hand. Essentially it's the gatekeeper for the senses and regulates what is processed by the brain. During meditation, thalamus activity is significantly reduced, allowing you to focus on your mindfulness. The way meditation affects each of these vital parts of the brain is quite amazing. It tends to help one make more sense of why they feel so much better after meditating as well.

Probably the most recognizable part of the brain is the grey matter. Whether you know much about what the grey matter does or not, you've most likely heard of it. But what exactly is the grey matter, and what effects does meditation have on this part of the brain? Grey matter is a type of neural tissue that's found in the brain and spinal cord. Grey matter regions are involved in sensory perception such as seeing and hearing, muscle control, speech, memory, emotions, self-control, and decision making. Essentially, it's basically responsible for most of what goes on in our central nervous system. Its role is vital in maintaining a healthy mind and body. So how does grey matter relate to meditation? Studies have shown that while meditating, the amount of grey matter in the frontal areas of the brain and in the hippocampus increases. An increase in brain matter can not only heighten our sense of well-being, but it can lead to more positive emotions, sharpen focus, and lead to longer-lasting emotional stability. Also, as we age, it's known that the density of our grey matter can diminish over time. Meditation has shown to help stop this loss of grey matter, thus keeping an aging brain healthier and sharper.

With all of the scientific and technical ways meditation can improve brain function, it's easy to overlook one of the more obvious ones, memory. The effects of mindful meditation have been linked to improving rapid memory recall. What this means is that those who meditate better are able to access their rapid memory, as well as recall and incorporate new facts. This is because when one has the ability to be in a state of mindfulness, they are able to adjust their brain waves and screen out the distractions that may otherwise cloud their recollection. By being in a state of relaxed focus, the brain is far more capable of processing what it's taking in and remembering that information. And with a better memory, you'll enjoy a sharper mind and more focus.

The information regarding meditation and the effects it has on the brain can be staggering. But once you can see past the scientific talk, it's easy to see that the benefits both mentally and physically are more than enough reason to give it a try. Not only will your body thank you, but so will your brain.

Chapter 7

Let's Cut to The Chase - How Do I Get Started?

So you've made the insightful decision to start meditating. Congratulations on starting your path to a more mindful, relaxing, and focused life! With this new venture into meditation will come questions such as, how do I get started? How do I know if I'm doing it right? And how do I know if it's working? While there really is no wrong or right way to mediate, it's natural to have these types of questions. It's important to realize that no matter the meditation technique, it all ends up coming from the same place, within your own mind and body. If you are thinking about picking up meditation, then you've already taken another step towards mindfulness. The first step was knowing that you are aware of mindfulness and want to be able to tap into it.

If you're apprehensive about just starting out, you may want to first try guided meditation. Guided meditation simply means that your meditation is done with an instructor or with instructional information. This type of meditation can either be done in a group or individually. If you feel comfortable in a calming atmosphere with other people seeking out their mindfulness as well, then group meditation may be perfect for you. On the other hand, if you'd prefer to meditate in solitude (which I personally subscribe), it may be better to do a guided meditation session in the comfort and privacy of your own home. In a group session, you'll have your own instructor who will talk you through your breathing and relaxing, and help get you focused on your mindfulness. It's a great way to be introduced to meditation if you're a little unsure about how and where to start. There is an abundance of resources one can find for helping with a guided meditation session. There are various books, DVDs, CDs, and websites that are great for starting out or for continuing to expand your meditational aspirations. These guided meditations for the individual self will help teach you proper meditation techniques, as well as help you determine what sort of meditation is the best fit for you. Whether you choose to do a group or individual guided session, it's a great way to be introduced to meditation and get a feel for the most beneficial ways to help you reach your mindfulness goals.

In addressing the question of knowing whether or not you are meditating the right way, the answer is quite simple. There truly is no wrong or right way. Each individual will have different methods and techniques they use in order to achieve the depth of mindfulness they're looking for. If you are following an authentic meditation technique, it's really quite difficult to be "doing it wrong" anyway. It's time to let go of the notion that there's a wrong way to meditate and embrace what comes most naturally for you and your mind. Making peace with the reality that your mind is going to wander from time to time is a good place to start when getting out of the mindset that maybe you're not meditating properly. On any given day, one can feel calm or distracted, peaceful or disturbed. The important thing is to realize that these are human attributes we all share, even those most disciplined in meditation. Don't be so hard on yourself. The less you sit evaluating your progress, the more time you'll be able to devote to establishing a meditation habit that will keep you more focused.

Some of the same things can be said in response to the question of wondering if meditation is working as wondering if you're doing it right. The two questions tend to go hand in hand. Meditation works on different levels for different people, depending on how long they've been doing it, what sort of meditation they practice, and how disciplined they are with keeping up with their mindfulness. An important notion to keep in mind is that the first few times around, you may have a hard time affirming if your meditation has been successful. You may need a few sessions to get a feel for it and find where you mind, body, and spirit need to be in order to reap all of the benefits from your meditations. However, if you're looking for some signs as to whether or not you're successfully meditating, there are a few key things that can be indicators that you are indeed in a state of mindfulness. In the first ten to fifteen minutes of meditation, it's quite common to experience a wide flurry of thoughts invading your mind. This may happen as you try to focus in on what you'll be meditating on. Eventually, you'll be able to tell your mind to calm down and settle in on the specific things you want to meditate on. Next, your breathing should become deeper and more regulated. As you feel your breaths becoming easier and deeper, it tends to be a sign that you're entering the first phase of meditation. Within in the next phase of meditation, you tend to lose track of your surroundings as you allow your mind to go even deeper into a mindful state. It's in this state of calm where your mind finds the serenity and objectivity to focus and relax. The most important thing to remember is to not give up on the meditation. If you feel as though it's not working for you, take in a deep breath and try again. Through repetition and perseverance, you'll gain the insight your mind needs for a proper meditation.

With each new meditation session you will notice subtle improvements in your awareness. Not necessarily this will happen linearly, but indeed it you will perceive incredible changes if you look at the bigger picture. Maybe your first three sessions were messy, but your fourth was simply amazing. Maybe your fifth is not quite good, but it's definitely better than the third. As a constant, you will continue to grow over the long term.

Getting started with meditation doesn't have to be a daunting ordeal. You've already taken the first steps towards a healthier mind and body by taking the initiative to want to meditate. From there it's about finding what types and techniques of meditation works best for you. It may take some trial and error, or you may be fortunate enough to find what works best for you right off the bat. Either way, have faith in your ability to achieve your desired mindfulness.

Always remember: meditation is a process. It's a journey, not a destination. The mere goal of meditating is the act of doing it. And with each session it goes by, things will get clearer and clearer. Improvements will become tangible. Undeniable. You just need time to see it.

Chapter 8

Meditation Tips to Get Started - How to Sit & How Long Each Session Should Last (With Pictures!)

When it comes to meditation, there are some helpful tips you can follow to help ensure you'll get all of the benefits possible out of your sessions. Keep in mind that these are general tips, so you can pretty much play with them. The important thing to remember is that these tips and guidelines are meant to help guide you in hopefully obtaining a more mindful and focused meditation session. Breathing technique, posture, focus, and when to meditate will be helpful in guiding you to having the ultimate meditation experience.

Of course, one of the main tips for meditation is to find a time that's most convenient for you. If you feel like you have to fit in the session or may be interrupted, you're not going to be able to fully immerse yourself into the mindfulness you need for a successful meditation. Not only is it important to set aside a time when you won't be interrupted, but it's also good to have your own special place to meditate. It's best to pick a place where you're least likely to be disturbed, and is a place of comfort and relaxation. Although some of those more experienced with meditation are able to better tune out the outside noises and distractions, it's probably best for a beginner to choose a place of quiet and solace. Feel free to make this space your own. It's all about what will make you feel the most relaxed and comfortable so you can get all you can out of your meditations.

There are two simple tips to follow before you start your meditation. Do not eat right before meditation, and be sure to wear comfortable clothing. It's best not to eat at least an hour before meditation because you'll risk feeling groggy or sluggish while your food is digesting and you're trying to find a state of mindfulness. But also, you shouldn't be hungry either. You don't want the distraction of a growling stomach while you're trying to focus on your meditation. As far as clothing goes, be sure to wear what's comfortable to you, something that will allow you to relax and allow for fluid movement if you're going to be doing a meditation with movement.

Stretching and posture are things to consider before you start your meditation. You may or may not choose to stretch before your session. Some like to do a few yoga moves before meditation in order to warm up the muscles and also get in a more peaceful frame of mind that will ease you into a smooth transition for meditation. If you don't really feel the need for stretching, that's fine too. You may want to just take the time to focus on your posture before you meditate then. There is no right or wrong way to sit or hold your posture during meditation. Like everything else involved, just be sure that you are comfortable and will be able to sit comfortably for a period of time so that your mind doesn't stray to an achy back or a foot falling asleep. Of course there is the traditional way of sitting for meditation, which is sitting with your legs crossed. The most important thing to remember is to be comfortable with how you're sitting. Keep your body relaxed and keep the focus on your meditation. A comfortable and erect posture should be maintained throughout your meditation session. Feel free to add a cushion to support your back or any other part of your body you think may tire while you are meditating. This will take the strain off your body, and keep your mind free from the distraction of a possible sore or strained body part.

Let's cut to the chase: How do I sit?

There are two important principles that you need to bear in mind in setting up a suitable posture for meditation:

- Your posture has to allow you to relax and to be comfortable

- Your posture has to allow you to remain alert and aware

Both of these are vitally important. If you're uncomfortable you'll not be able to meditate because of discomfort. If you can't relax then you won't be able to enjoy the meditation practice and, just as importantly, you won't be able to let go of the underlying emotional conflicts that cause your physical tension.

From reading that, you might well think that it would be best to meditate lying down. Bad idea! If you're lying down your mind will be foggy at best, and you may well even fall asleep. If you've ever been to a yoga class that ends with shavasana (the corpse pose), where people lie on the floor and relax, you'll have noticed that about a third of the class is snoring within five minutes. Forget about meditating lying down. The best way to effectively combine relaxation AND awareness is a sitting posture. You don't have to sit cross-legged, or even sit on the floor.

We'll show you how to set up an effective posture in three positions: sitting in a chair, sitting astride a cushion or on a stool, and sitting cross-legged. All of these work: the important thing is to find one in which you will be comfortable.

Remember: you may think it looks really cool to sit cross-legged, but if you don't have the flexibility it takes to do that then you'll simply suffer! Make it easy on yourself. Choose a posture that is right for you.

Before we dive into different meditation postures, let's see the most important aspects of sitting properly:

1. Your spine should be upright, following its natural tendency to be slightly hollowed. You should neither be slumped nor have an exaggerated hollow in your lower spine.

2. Your spine should be relaxed.

3. Your shoulders should be relaxed, and slightly rolled back and down.

4. Your hands should be supported, either resting on a cushion or on your lap, so that your arms are relaxed.

5. Your head should be balanced evenly, with your chin slightly tucked in. The back of your neck should be relaxed, long, and open.

6. Your face should be relaxed, with your brow smooth, your eyes relaxed, your jaw relaxed, and your tongue relaxed and just touching the back of your teeth.

Take your position

Just as a tree needs to set down deep roots so it won't fall over as it grows, you need to find a comfortable position for the lower half of your body that you can sustain for 5 or 10 or 15 minutes — or even longer, if you wish. After several millennia of experimentation, the great meditators have come up with a handful of traditional postures that seem to work especially well. Different though they may appear from the outside, these postures have one thing in common: the pelvis tilts slightly forward, accentuating the natural curvature of the lower back.

The following poses are arranged more or less in order, from the easiest to the hardest to do, though ease all depends on your particular body and degree of flexibility. For example, some people take to the classical *lotus* position (whose name derives from its resemblance to the flower) like a duck to . . . well, to a lotus pond. Besides, the lotus, though difficult, has some definite advantages, and you can work up to it.

- **Sitting in a chair:** The trick to meditating in a chair is positioning your buttocks somewhat higher than your knees, which tilts your pelvis forward and helps keep your back straight. (See Figure 1.) Old-fashioned wooden kitchen chairs work better than the upholstered kind; experiment with a small cushion or foam wedge under your buttocks. Don't slouch.

Figure 1: Position your buttocks a bit higher than your knees.

- **Kneeling (with or without a bench):** This technique was popular in ancient Egypt and in traditional Japan where it's called *seiza* (see Figure 2.). Kneeling can be — well, hard on your knees, unless you have proper support. Try placing a cushion under your buttocks and between your feet — or use a specially designed seiza bench, preferably one with a soft cushion between you and the wood. Otherwise, your bottom and other tender parts may fall asleep.

Figure 2: Kneeling can be hard on your knees, so try to add some cushioning.

- **Easy position:** Not recommended for extended periods of sitting because it's not very stable and doesn't support a straight spine. Simply sit on your cushion with your legs crossed in front of you tailor-fashion. (Believe it or not, tailors once sat this way!) Your knees don't have to touch the floor, but do keep your back as straight as you can.

You can stabilize the position by placing cushions under your knees; gradually decrease the height of the cushions as your hips become more flexible (which they naturally will over time). When your knees touch the ground, you may be ready for Burmese or lotus position (see later bullets for these positions).

This pose can be a short-term alternative for people who can't manage the other positions in this list, can't kneel because of knee problems, or don't want to sit on a chair for some reason.

- **Burmese position:** This pose, shown in Figure 3, is used throughout Southeast Asia. This pose involves placing both calves and feet on the floor one in front of the other. Although less stable than the lotus series, it's much easier to negotiate, especially for beginners.

Figure 3: The Burmese position is good for beginners.

With all the cross-legged poses, first bend your leg at the knee, in line with your thigh, before rotating your thigh to the side. Otherwise, you risk injuring your knee, which is built to flex in only one direction, unlike the ball-and-socket joint of the hip, which can rotate through a full range of motion.

- **Quarter lotus:** Exactly like the half lotus, except that your foot rests on the calf of your opposite leg, rather than on the thigh.

- **Half lotus:** Easier to execute than the famous full lotus, and nearly as stable (see Figure 4). With your buttocks on a cushion, place one foot on the opposite thigh and the other foot on the floor beneath the opposite thigh. Be sure that both knees touch the floor and your spine doesn't tilt to one side. To distribute the pressure on your back and legs, remember to alternate legs from sitting to sitting, if you can — in other words, left leg on the thigh, right on the floor, then left on the floor and right on the thigh.

Figure 4: Both knees should touch the floor in the half lotus.

- **Full lotus:** Considered the Everest of sitting positions (see Figure 5). With your buttocks on a cushion, cross your left foot over your right thigh and your right foot over your left thigh. As with its more asymmetrical sibling, half lotus, it's best to alternate legs in order to distribute the pressure evenly.

Full lotus has been practiced throughout the world for many thousands of years. The most stable of all the poses, it should not be attempted unless you happen to be particularly flexible — and even then you should preparing by doing some stretches.

Figure 5: The full lotus is the "Everest" of sitting positions.

How long should each session last?

A question that may arise before beginning a meditation routine is how long you should meditate for. While the length of time one meditates for will vary from person to person, you may want to start out with shorter sessions and then gradually work your way up to longer meditations. You may find that your mind is only able to focus for a certain amount of time. If that's the case, then you'll want to choose shorter meditations. Once you get the hang of things, it will become easier to train your mind to meditate longer. The key is to be patient and allow yourself to work up to more prolonged meditations. It's also good to get into a routine for your meditation. Be consistent when you meditate. When a routine is established, you'll be able to devote ample time needed for your meditations. Typically, a mediation session of twenty to thirty minutes is sufficient. Listen to what your mind and body is telling you. It will know when you've reached your peak of mindfulness.

Breathing is an important component of meditation. Before you begin your session, you'll be mindful of your breathing, but eventually, as you get deeper into your meditation, the breathing will meld with your mindfulness and become a part of your mind and body. When you begin your meditation, focus on your breathing. This means be aware that you're breathing, know that you're breathing. Feel the rise and fall of your chest and the sensation of air filling your lungs and leaving as you exhale. Realize that breathing is a natural part of everything and is essential to your mindfulness. Develop your own breathing routine. Play around with what works and what doesn't, and you'll end up finding the perfect pattern of breathing that is conducive to your own mindfulness. Always remember that meditation is exercise for your brain, and like any type of exercise, your breathing is very important.

Another great tip to help with your meditation is how to deal with your emotions. We can't always have days where we can sit down and fall into our meditation without some sort of emotion whirling through our minds. And it's going to be difficult to settle into a meditation if your emotions aren't in check. Feelings such as anger, shame, and fear tend to resonate the strongest in our minds. One of the best ways to release these emotions for your meditation is to just go with them. Focus on what your body is feeling in regards to those emotions. For example, fear could be this feeling of a tight band around your chest. Focusing on that physical feeling and letting your mind work through it will help get your mind and body cleared of these emotions. Eventually you'll be free of these feelings that stand in the way of a clear meditation and you'll be focused on finding your mindfulness.

By using these tips and listening to your body and mind, you're well on your way to a successful meditation plan. Just remember to stick with it, and let your mindfulness fall into place.

Chapter 9

How Do I Build Upon A Meditation Habit? - Make It Long Term!

With all of the strategies provided on how to start meditating and how you can benefit from it, the next hurdle to overcome is how to stick with meditation over the long term. If you're not one to keep up with a goal or something you've started, it's important to find a meditation routine you're happy with and keep doing it. Meditation is not for those looking for instant gratification. It's a practice in patience and mindfulness, and its benefits will only be unlocked by the perseverant mind. This is why meditation, although being a great tool obtain relatively quick results (relaxation, increased focus, inner calmness), should be incorporated on your daily schedule over the long term in order to reap all its fruits.

So many have people have attested to the power of meditation and how it has played a vital role in changing their lives. Some have said it's the most powerful thing they've ever learned. Those types of statements alone should help influence you to keep up with your meditation habit. And one of the most amazing things about meditation is that it's really one of the simplest habits to build! It's not every day that one finds a healthy habit, one that will nourish the mind, body and soul. One of the things most people don't realize, however, is that having a meditation habit could be vital in improving or getting rid of other habits that aren't exactly beneficial to one's health.

Harness the power of Balance & Momentum

We have all been there: too much work, too little social life (or maybe even the other way around). Too much mental efforts, close to none physical training. Do you get where I'm going? Yes, I'm talking about balance.

Don't get me wrong: I do understand that balance can fade away on the short term in order to focus your energies exclusively on the task at hand. I've even once thought that one could live that way, but guess what? I was wrong. Although an unbalanced life can be tolerated for a while, it's no far from being a long term strategy. Especially if you care about living a long, happy, stress free life.

What does this all have to do with willpower, you may ask? Actually, a lot. Enduring self control can only be achieved if you are happy with your life. If you are not, then trying to –in top of everything else- get disciplined to do things you'd rather not do is a living hell on earth. It just can't be done on the long term.

Happiness is indeed one key aspect of highly disciplined people. Nevertheless, discipline and happiness are far from being the same thing: we all know somewhat happy people whose willpower is so weak that it makes me cry just to think about it. At the same time, you may even know some sad people who despite being unhappy manage to get their "to do lists" right on time.

But know what? The key is this: happiness without self-discipline and self discipline without happiness are both unsustainable over the long term. We need to be able to discipline ourselves to do things we'd rather not to right away in order to accomplish higher goals, while at the same time enjoy the road. Is that too much to ask? Of course not!

I known both you and I are trying to get a different kind of happiness from the "undisciplined happy person". You have picked up this book for a reason: you are willing to fight for the good things in life, not just take whatever it's thrown to you. That is why you need both, and in order to do that, why don't just make the road easier? It's all about setting the proper ground so that you can achieve all the things you know you can achieve.

I want you to find balance in your life, expanding in every possible way. Why should you? Simple: because there is a physical law that will help you out if you do. And if you don't, the same law will get back to you and attack you with all its power.

I'm talking about momentum. It works like this: as long as you are expanding, the subsequent improvements you set yourself up to will get easier. They will just flow. Think of it like riding a bicycle: at first it's hard, but once you get on going, movement replicates itself.

The same happens with self discipline. Once you get down to fight for what you want in life, each subsequent goal will get easier to achieve. Once you discipline yourself to exercise daily, taking up meditation will be almost effortless. Even more, once you've tackled exercising and meditation, eating the right foods will feel just natural. Further on, building a healthy lifestyle will get easier and easier.

At the same time, if your life is filled with crappy habits, they will replicate themselves. Just like a riding a bicycle, only that this time you'll be riding backwards. If you engage in behaviors that actually erode your willpower, what do you think will happen with your life in general? Each time you miss the gym you are not just "skipping one training session", you are actually destroying the self discipline you've worked so hard to develop! Once you do, you will be much more likely to skip the next meditation routine, and you'll probably end up eating garbage the next day. It's a physical law: there is no way around it. You just need to be aware of it so that you can use it in your favor!

Movement will replicate movement of the same kind. What kind that is it's up to you. Never forget this!

With our busy lives and hectic lifestyles, it's easy to make excuses as to why we don't have the time to keep up with a meditation routine. Maybe you can't make the time, perhaps you're too comfortable plopped on the couch in front of the television, or maybe you're buried in a mountain of paperwork for your job. Whatever the excuse may be, there's a simple solution: Make it easy so that you can't say no. While that may sound way too easy to be true, think about what its saying. When you start small and simple, you'll eventually work your way into keeping up with your habit, in this case meditation, and want to build upon your skills.

Starting out small is the key to incorporating a healthy habit into your lifestyle. With meditation, it's a matter of finding a time that works best for you, keeping your sessions short to begin with, and maintaining a schedule that keeps meditation in your daily routine. If you want to meditate, it's important that you do it on a regular basis. Before long, you'll realize that it's become second nature to get into your meditations.

When trying to maintain a meditation habit, it's important to be mindful of the negative thoughts that might be in your head. It's those negative thoughts that will try to sabotage the meditation habit that you've already tried to establish. A good example would be somebody who's trying to quit a smoking habit. Though they may be unaware of it, the stress or emotions of a long day or something that happened may take over their mind with negative emotions. When that happens, they will tend to make excuses for breaking their healthy habit. In the case of the smoker, they might tell themselves, what's one cigarette going to hurt? Although equating meditation with smoking is not in the same realm of healthiness, if you let your negative thoughts invade your mind, you'll find yourself putting off your meditation. Maybe it's only for a day. Then you'll find yourself making excuses for the next day and before you know it, you're not meditating at all anymore. These negative thoughts can be very tempting and powerful. But as you've come to realize, the power of meditation is even greater. Never underestimate the power your mind has over your will to do something, especially if that something is as beneficial as meditation. Leave those negative thoughts at the door and get in the good habit of not making excuses.

A great way to keep up with your meditation routine is to savor the habit. In other words, look forward to it and indulge in every moment you are in your state of mindfulness. Be aware of what you're experiencing when you meditate. By being aware of how the mediation is relaxing your mind, body, and spirit, you're going to want keep up with your sessions. As humans, we crave what makes us feel good, and as you indulge in the goodness that comes from meditation, you'll begin to realize that it should be a part of your daily healthy habits.

So what happens if you do fall off track with your meditation habit? It's important to remember to not be too hard on yourself. Things happen and sometimes we get caught up in the business of our lives. So have a plan when you falter with getting in your meditation. First, you need to make sure you re-start if you do falter. If it's been a few days, be sure to not let it go much longer and get back into your routine. Just be sure not to go past three days. Studies have found that missing one day is nothing too drastic, missing two days isn't exactly great, but you'll manage to recover, but after missing three days, the habit is pretty much shot. A great way to keep up with your meditation habit is get some accountability. Perhaps you will want to give yourself some sort of reward for keeping up with your sessions. Maybe at the end of the week you can treat yourself to dinner at your favorite restaurant. It's all about what motivates you to stick with your meditation habit. If you're having a bit of trouble with maintaining your habit, you can recruit a friend or family member to help hold you accountable. Perhaps for every day you miss a meditation, you must give this person a certain amount of money or have to do them a favor. Your motivation lies in not having to be held accountable and therefore you'll be sure to keep up with your meditations.

How Do Habits Form?

Habits (whether good or bad) form when a particular action (or set of actions) is performed repeatedly. They may feel unnatural to you at first, but with time, you get used to the actions and those actions become habit.

Habits are the mind's way of making sure that you can do certain things without thinking about them in an effort to become more productive. However, when bad habits form this way, they can turn your life into one of being less productive and efficient.

For instance, if you normally go without breakfast in the morning, you have become used to the habit of not eating in the morning.

However, if you start eating a slice of toast every morning before you go to work, you will find that, at first, it feels unusual to be doing this. If you stick with the routine, though, you will soon see that having this slice of toast has become a habit. This is because you do it every day.

The same can be said for someone who has never smoked before. When they smoke that first cigarette, it feels weird, but after repeated efforts, that person will soon make a habit of smoking (whether it is one a day or several an hour) – the habit will form.

The actual act of repeating something causes your brain to connect the situation with the action – so for instance, feeling stressful may cause you to smoke. You learn to associate smoking with stressful situations and vice versa.

If you really want to make a change, then try to focus on what is causing the habit and focus on the things you can do to improve that cause – don't focus on the habit itself.

An example here could be that you want to master the habit of eating more healthily. However, if you find that every time you become stressed or emotionally overwhelmed, you indulge in pizza and chocolate bars and, as a result, you feel comforted and happy; then trying to replace those things with things like eating more green vegetables and drinking vegetable juice will not fix the problem.

What you need to do is find a different way of calming yourself down when you become stressed or too emotional. In its simplicity, you need to generate the same feelings you get when eating pizza and chocolate, but you must do so in a way which is better for you, your health and your wellbeing.

When you can do this, you will soon find that you probably aren't eating as much junk food as you were before.

The bottom line when it comes to forming and keeping up with the meditation habit is simply just to do it. If you have to force yourself to keep up with it at the start, then so be it. Even if it takes simplifying your meditation habits to be able to fit it in everyday, you're still accomplishing and establishing a healthy habit of mindfulness. It's always important to keep your focus and maintain a schedule that works for you. Don't be discouraged if things don't seem to be working right away. As with all things meditation, patience is the key. Take your time, work yourself into a routine that fits your lifestyle, and you're sure to keep the healthy and mindful habit that is meditation.

Chapter 10

Tying Everything Into A Glorious Know - How Meditation Will Work For You

With so much information to absorb about the types of meditation, what sort of meditation will be right for you, and figuring out how to maintain a steady meditation habit, it's normal to be overwhelmed. It can be a lot to take it, but it doesn't have to be a complicated process. The path to finding your road to mindfulness will lead to an awakening of your mind, body, and spirit. With the patience and the knowledge, you're bound to find what works best for you.

Remember that meditation is surrender. It's about surrendering your stresses, your worries, your fears, and all of the negative emotions that are holding you back from living your life fully. When you meditate, you're nourishing your mind. And when your mind is nourished, the rest of your body will fall into sync. If you're more of the religious or spiritual type, you can think of meditation as fuel for your spiritual growth. And since meditation has been around since ancient times, it has quite an impressive track record when it comes to changing lives.

If you tend to lead a stressful lifestyle, you've already learned about what that kind of thing can do to your body. Stress is an everyday part of life, but it doesn't have to be something that consumes you and wreaks havoc on your mind and body. Think of that stress as a plague. Not only a physical plague, but a mental one as well. The longer you let it run its course through your body, the worse off you're going to be. Meditation is a proven way to battle this stress and help eliminate it from your life. Through mediation, you'll gain a mindfulness that will help you put a healthy distance between you and that stress that tends to take over your thoughts. Through meditation, you'll be able to see things clearly, as if you're seeing that distance you've put between you and the stress, and will be able to successfully let it go.

You may be wondering how mediation is going to be different from the other things and techniques you may have tried in order to achieve a feeling of balance in your life. How is meditation set apart from just simply relaxing, thinking, concentration, or practicing self-hypnosis? Meditation is different from these other forms of mental exercise because it's truly relaxing to the brain. Not only does it relax us, but it infuses our minds and bodies with optimism, peace, and joy. Not only that, but it can transform us from being the typical over-stressed and tired human, to more deeply beautiful and enriched persons. Mindfulness is a powerful thing. And being able to use that mindfulness to enhance and better one's life is a truly humbling experience.

Don't forget to remember what the main purposes of meditation are. If you're seeking out a more relaxed state of mind, then you already have your reason and incentive for deciding to incorporate mindfulness into your everyday life. Meditation is getting your mind and body into a state of silence. Nothing else exists aside from your focus on the calm and serene. It's in this silence that we can look inside ourselves with an introspect that has no pride, no guilt, no fears, and no stress. Through mediation, we can extend far beyond mere relaxation. We can experience an awareness where we are not weighed down by the thoughts of anxiety, stress, and negative emotion plaguing our conscious minds. By being in the presence of our own minds, we are able to experience our true nature and find a peace and focus we may never have known existed within us had we continued down a path absent of mindfulness.

Embrace meditation as your own. Don't think of it as something you have to do or are forced to partake in. You'll be missing the whole point of finding your mindfulness and focus for a clearer and more relaxed mind. You cannot force meditation. Let it come to you. Once again, patience is the essence of allowing yourself to be fully immersed in the innumerable benefits meditation can bestow upon you. Meditation is not something you can buy or sell. It's not something you can hope to learn through shortcuts or only going through the motions and not fully committing yourself to mindfulness. It's also important to dispel all of the myths you may have about meditation from your mind before starting your own routine. If you go into it thinking you're going to have some sort of miraculous experience that is nothing short of a spiritual miracle, then you're seeking out meditation for all the wrong reasons. Keep it simple and eventually you'll get to where you need to be with your focus and mindfulness.

Above all else, when making the decision to start meditating, know that you are well on your way to finding your inner beauty and peace. The ability to love oneself as well as other fellow human beings is one of the most beautiful qualities we have as human beings. With meditation, we have the ability and capacity to trigger this trait more deeply and spiritually. When we are able to find our inner happiness and beauty from within as an individual, we are able to take that and practice it with others. Through meditation and your mindfulness, you'll see the world in a different way. It will be a more positive, inviting, beautiful, and stress free place. This comes from being aware of your inner focus and being able to channel that peace and apply it to your everyday life. When we are in a calmer, more peaceful, and more focused state of mind, we are able to have a positive influence on those around us. And because the key to all of this positivity comes from incorporating meditation into our lives, there's no question that it will change your life for the better.

Chapter 11

Proving You're a Buddhist When You Don't Even Know It

A study in 2012 by "Yoga in America" confirmed it: over 20 million Americans regularly practice yoga. In 2008, that number was 15 million. There aren't numbers new enough for this year, but you can bet it's progressing at a similarly healthy rate. Yoga studios line city streets, yoga mats are in every female freshman student's dorm, yoga classes are available everywhere.

Yoga is no, strictly speaking, a Buddhist practice. It's more derived from Hinduism, a more ancient Indian religion that ran alongside Buddhism as competing or intertwining beliefs around a thousand years ago. The relationship between Hinduism and Buddhism is very, very complicated, so we won't expand on that here; suffice it to say Hinduism is the one with all the gods (Vishnu, Shiva, etc.) and there have been many meshes throughout Southeast Asia between the two philosophies.

Yoga is very, very old, so old that the original Supreme Buddha—Gautama himself—did yoga. (Of course, it was during his "still haven't found what I'm looking for" phase of six years, but still—yoga's old.)

So while it's a stretch to call yoga of a piece with Buddhism, or vice versa, the similarities exist, and if you already do yoga—and, frankly speaking, if you're a middle-class women of any amount of privilege in North America there's a decent chance that you do—there are good reasons to investigate further Buddhist teachings.

How Do They Overlap?

Just as Buddhist meditation aims to guide our minds towards personal mindfulness—namely, this is the desire sought when we perform the Mindfulness of Breathing meditation—yoga, too, strives to make us more aware of how our bodies feel and move.

Yoga draws attention to our physical bodies, so that we are able to explore our corporeal lives more thoroughly. For example, after stretching and performing yogic acts, we are ideally more adept at sitting still and being calm. Yoga aims to reduce the stress and lethargy in our lives. It is a sort of purification of our purely physical restlessness.

This is not unlike Buddhist meditation. The key theme is that both offer you the tool needed to explore hidden depths of your mind and be mindful of the logical paths our minds take.

Both also aim to complete our lives on a spiritual level. While the teachings of the Supreme Buddha are more thorough and expansive (and, obviously, have shot off into a million other philosophies) and yoga does emphasize physical awareness more, both share very similar pillars of how to be a good person. The philosophies behind both rely on karma, clarity of sight and an end to the suffering we all inevitably feel.

Many Buddhists find yoga helpful—on a base level, because it helps them sit still longer to meditate, but also on a deeper level.

Because both yoga and Buddhism deal with mindfulness of the body rather than metaphysical realities, they couple one another very nicely with regards to pinpointing personal sensations within the body. They force you to stop and think about your body intimately and uniquely, which we rarely get a chance to do when we constantly distract ourselves with material matters.

There isn't just overlap in the Western world, also. Many of the world's significant Buddhist leaders were once worrying that the attraction so many Westerners have to both yoga and Buddhism was more material—yoga is sexy, Buddhism makes you spiritual, and so forth.

But in fact that's not the case. There are several Zen monestaries in Japan that are introducing yoga to their daily rituals. The precision of yoga helps Buddhists learn absorption in their own practices. Many modern day Buddhists perform yoga because they find it simply complements their own belief system perfectly; the two can come off as a natural fit. This becomes even more evidence when you read the literature behind both beliefs and notice the similarities—differences exist too, of course, but once you engage with both on an intellectual level as well as a spiritual one, you're already enveloping yourself in Buddhist doctrine.

None of this is to mention the fact that, above all, the dharma—the teachings of the Supreme Buddha—are migrating westward with tangible results and followers, not just superficial ones. One of the offshoots of yogic practice is that people are genuinely starting to pay attention to East and Southeast Asian religions, more and more. Integration is a reality. Others might call it "globalization". Great American authors of the 19th century like

Ralph Waldo Emerson and Henry David Thoreau were familiar with Buddhist scripture, and though they are very stereotypically American authors, their sense of belonging to nature, and their drives towards isolation and feeling at peace with their own minds derives heavily from the teachings of the Supreme Buddha dharma.

If I Do Yoga, Should I Try Meditating? Or vice versa?

That's a difficult question—partly because to practice yogic stances *is* a form of meditation. It's not a Buddhist form, but it is still a form. So while the answer is "probably yes," you should only attempt either if you feel you know what you want out of it.

If you don't do yoga yet, it's worth a shot. Many people find yoga helpful for a number of reasons, not the least of which are physical health reasons—yoga keeps us limber and helps our blood flow. There are variations, too, such as hot yoga, which takes place in a sauna-like environment and encourages you to sweat out toxins from your pores.

Many others enjoy the peacefulness of holding a position for an extended period of time. The ability to stop and feel breathing happening in your body, which is essential to both yoga and Buddhism, is an invaluable learning experience.

Yoga mats are very affordable and available almost everywhere now. YouTube clips of yogis, both professional and amateur, are ubiquitous. You don't even have to leave your bedroom. Honestly, if you're skeptical of the whole thing, the best course of action is to simply give it a shot and see if you feel different afterward. Part of the challenge is physical ability, but more of it is mental. To overcome a hesitation about yoga is in and of itself a Buddhist advancement, proving that you can overcome your overbearing sense of self-righteous ego and are willing to work towards becoming a fuller, happier human being.

Chapter 12

Karma, Rebirth, Rinse, Repeat

Anyone who's done a good deed, listened to Radiohead or even just browsed Reddit has heard the word before: "Karma." But what exactly is it?

Karma is a key notion to Buddhism, and one of its most central, fundamental and far-reaching concepts. Yet it is also one of the most heatedly discussed and often disputed concepts.

Karma as we know it, as Westerners have appropriated it, refers to the idea that *what we do now will affect us in the future*. So if you're a bratty, obnoxious, despicable person who is all kinds of selfish and greedy and miserable to others, the law of karma dictates that your life will go sour soon—or, worse still, that your next life will be as, say, a slave, in order for you to learn humility.

Karma ties in deeply with the theme of rebirth, or reincarnation. Buddha believed that we are all reborn again and again until we reach ultimate enlightenment and attain a sense of nirvana. It's like a video game: when you die, you simply restart at the beginning and try again.

Now, personally speaking, I find that one of the most comforting approaches to death of any religion out there. No eternal heaven and hell; no dozens of virgins waiting in the clouds. Just reach ultimate personal happiness and comfort.

What's that? Didn't quite make it? Don't worry; just try again.

Defining "Karma"

Literally, the translation of karma means "action". It's meant to refer to the fact that every action has a consequence. This is sometimes referred to as a butterfly effect—that a butterfly flapping its wings now will create a gust of wind so strong it becomes a hurricane across the world.

Karma is both a creator of the future and a descriptor of the past. It is a combination of our intentions, actions and thoughts. When people try to predict karma, however, they come to lead repetitive lives. This isn't particularly healthy. It transforms us into cyclical beings who repeat our failures, or become pre-conditioned automatons. That's why the goal is to avoid karma altogether by reaching enlightenment.

A common symbol of karma in East and Southeast Asia is the lotus flower. If you visit these any temples in these East or Southeast Asian countries, you might see a lotus flower floating in a still pond or a small pool of water. A blooming lotus is one of the few flowers in existence that, while it blossoms, carries seeds inside itself. Get the metaphor? The seeds are the past, the creation of the flower; the flower itself is the blooming future unfolding before itself. It's a perfect symbol.

And yet, the exact definition of karma has become something of a touchy subject. This is because so many use karma as an excuse for why their lives are bad: "Oh, my back is always aching; I must have lived a bad life in the past." This mode of thinking alleviates oneself from any responsibility and doesn't allow for progress. You're still blaming and not accepting reality.

Some argue that while karma strictly translates to "action—which it does, technically—it actually refers more to intentions. I once read an article in a psychology magazine about how karma is the definition of our intentions at any given moment. The argument, then, is that wielding a knife is too vague an action to condemn or praise: what if it's a surgeon wielding it to save a life? What if it's a robber trying to mug someone? What if it's a man trying to untie a tough knot?

In this case, intention defines karma. Good intentions make for good karma, and bad intentions make for bad karma.

But it isn't so simple, even still. Because good intentions can still result in bad behavior. I could intend to be kind when I tell my friend she looks fat in that dress—after all, she does, and she asked my opinion—but I did not anticipate the hurt that she would feel when I said that. Do I get good karma for wanting to help, or bad karma for hurting my friend?

There are so many specific instances of difficult moral dilemmas, so often explored in philosophy, religion and the arts, that it would seem impossible to rate them all. That's why, ultimately, the goal of karma is not to improve your life exponentially. You should not be a good person for the sake of good karma—if this is the case, then you're being selfish in only acting kindly for the benefit of your future self.

Rather, the benefit of karma is to extend beyond it. Nirvana, the ultimate goal in Buddhism, lies not with conventional good deeds—although things like donating to charity and being supporting and saying Loving Kindness mantras do help others—but instead with personal self-satisfaction. You want to be, for lack of a better or more applicable phrase, in a "Zen state of mind".

Part of that, however, means necessarily thinking good and pure thoughts. In order to affect positivity and mindfulness, the Supreme Buddha taught that people should imbue their own thoughts with good will. We must train our minds the way we might train a dog—the more goodness we think, the more likely we are to think good thoughts, and the more genuinely kind our actions will be.

If the kindness of our actions is born not out of greed but out of a genuine spirit, then the purification of our souls can be regarded as sincere.

How Serious is All of This?

The fact is that nobody knows for sure. Like I mentioned above, the Chinese government created a specific law making illegal reincarnation. So obviously enough Chinese bureaucrats believe this to be a real thing. How do we know if we're ever reborn? How can we scientifically prove the existence of good or bad karma?

Well, there's obviously no hard scientific proof—in much the same way that no religion is founded on scientific truth, but rather out of firm belief and philosophical study. There's a logic to

Buddhism, the same way there's a logic to Christianity, Judaism or Islam. Each sect, or tradition, has developed their own justification for these theories. Some Mahayana Buddhist masters might define rebirth different from Zen Buddhist masters.

One convincing argument is that we should live our lives *as if karma exists*, and truly convince ourselves of that fact, because it is simply a good way to live. Even if the end is not nirvana or a good next life, but only a pleasant and moral life *this* time around, is that such a bad thing? (God forbid, the only benefit is that you're a good person for the rest of your life!)

Buddhists are strangely pragmatic in this light. Because there is so much uncertainty, it increases their faith. The less we know for sure, the more we should assume belief. The less we know, the more we should trust.

It's beginning to sound a lot like some other religions I can think of...

Another famous interpretation is by a famous monk who concluded that the concept of life and rebirth is just to appeal to mass Buddhists, to make Buddhism digestible. In truth, the Supreme Buddha may have meant that each "life" and "death" was of the ego rising up within ourselves, into our minds. In this light, we are born again, and die again, several times in a day; the benefit to good karma isn't a whole other life, but rather a happy emotional state—doing good makes you feel good, and acting badly causes guilt and sorrow.

And you know what? At the end of the day, isn't that what life is about? Do good deeds, and virtue is its own reward. Live a sinful life and you'll live with guilt. Another relevant quotation from the Supreme Buddha himself: "Should a person do good, let him do it again and again. Let him find pleasure therein, for blissful is the accumulation of good."

Suddenly, Buddhism doesn't feel so foreign anymore.

At the end of the day, it's your decision. Many choose to interpret karma in their own personal way to live a happier, more fulfilling life. There's no right or wrong. There's no heaven or hell. There's an ultimate nirvana, but the odds of you reaching it this time around and becoming a fully-fledged Bodhisattva are frankly pretty slim. More likely, you'll just become a better person.

So take from the Supreme Buddha's teachings what you will—in the end, he was only trying to help you out.

Chapter 13

Living In The Present Moment (Hey, It's All There Is)

Be honest, now: how stressed out are you? What's on your mind? What's bothering you? Is it your mortgage? Your kids' grades? Unable to find the right job? Are you single? Are you terminally ill? Did you just forget your iPhone in the pocket of your jeans when you put them in the washing machine, and now are dreading having to buy a new phone and post on Facebook that you need every one of your friends' phone numbers again because you never memorized a single one?

Literally none of the above problems mean you should be unhappy now. And why is that? Because none deal with the *present moment*, which is an essential Buddhist teaching.

You hear this a lot when reading up on Buddhism: *Live in the now, enjoy the moment, don't take life for granted.* A quote often misattributed to the Supreme Buddha (but not actually originally said by him) goes along the lines of, "*The secret of health for both mind and body is not to mourn for the past or worry about the future, but to live in the present moment wisely and earnestly.*"

The Buddha might not have said it, but he'd probably agree with it.

In examining all of life's problems—and we can start with the ones cited above as examples—we have to boil them down to what *really* bothers us. Why should our kids' grades matter, for example? An "F" on an essay in and of itself means little. But there might be multiple worries here: that you feel you failed as a parent, you didn't study with your child enough or didn't emphasize the importance of education—in other words, you're worried about *past actions*—or else you're concerned about your child's *future*, whether this trend of failure will continue, whether he or she will be successful or live a promising, fulfilling life.

We have no immediate power to change any of those—the past has passed, and the future has yet to come. The best we can do is act in the now. Following this example, all you can do, rather than mourn the past or stress over the future, is approach your child and have a frank discussion about grades. Help him or her with homework *today*. When tomorrow comes, do it again.

Our problems almost always deal with the past and future, and very rarely with the present. It's an unhealthy approach to life.

Stress almost necessarily exists in the future or past—we regret bad decisions or fear upcoming ones. And stress, as science has proven, is well-documented to lead to an unhealthy lifestyle; it is a subtle cause of heart problems and physical illnesses.

So how do we stop thinking about the past and future? How do we simply "live in the present moment"?

It starts by accepting your current place in the world. Dreams aren't dangerous, but they can be delusional if you live within them too often. Having a life goal is a strong driver to get up in the mornings. But living in a future fantasy isn't helpful, and focusing on it too much—instead of concerning yourself with present matters—can lead to ignoring your friends and family, placing too much stress on your career and simply not enjoying yourself. Instead of worrying about your family in the future, enjoy the family you have now. Instead of worrying about how you might lose your friends in a big move to another city, hang out with the friends you *can* see.

When you stop worrying about the past and present, it is easier to live a life of no regrets. You can live comfortably, knowing that every decision you made, you made with the utmost knowledge you had at that time. You made decisions you can stand by. There's no reason to feel bad about that.

Falling into the "I'll do it tomorrow" trap is also essential to avoid if you want to be a happier person. This isn't a black-and-white issue, of course: say you want to quit your job and travel the world for a year, but you don't have any money. Obviously you have to plan for the future. It's not a contradiction to plan for the future if you're at least planning *today*. Don't expect it all to fall into place 12 months from now: start saving up money every single day with your ultimate goal in mind. Act today to create your future in the present.

This is an essential Buddhist teaching. Meditation, yoga, karmic good deeds—all point to how we need to be *more aware of ourselves now*, more in tune with our day-to-day lives, and less concerned with our pasts or futures. You have to relax your mind, because *the past and future only exist in your mind*. There is, literally and physically, no other moment that exists than right now. Stress only exists in your mind. Regret only exists in your mind.

What meditation teaches us—especially the breathing meditation—is that we must be aware of every part of ourselves in this very moment. "Clearing your mind" is the key concept. Yoga teaches this, too, by forcing us to focus all our mental energies on our physical bodies, and move slowly, feeling what is happening to our bodies as it is happening. If our minds are miles away, thinking about what to cook for dinner or what dress to wear to a big party this weekend, the meditative powers of both meditation and yoga fall flat.

That's why living in the moment requires such mental fitness. We're constantly distracting ourselves with planning and worrying. Our minds are scattershot—especially in an age of bills, rent, socializing and mass media, not to mention our own physical health and careers, we are subjected constantly to a myriad problems with no way to focus our minds on all at once. Our minds are messy.

So, what's a good way to start living in the moment?

You already know—you read it in this book.

The ultimate take away from this book, I hope, has been that everything is guiding you to experience yourself in a more pure and honest way than you had been before.

Remember what mindfulness teaches us: to be constantly self-aware of your present condition, the flow of your thoughts, the feeling of breathing in and out, the state of your corporeal self.

Mindful meditation forces us to sit still and think only about our present moment. It is essential training for a life of contentment.

Remember what Buddhism teaches us: to be aware of our bodies, to block out the rest of the world, to exist in a Zen state of mind and spend some time learning how your body works.

And, of course, remember what karma teaches us: to be good people, regardless of our past and, most importantly, *regardless of the future.* Don't live life for some future payoff that may never happen. Live life for what you can achieve now, today, by yourself and on your own terms. Live to be happy today.

Conclusion

You Don't Need to Be a Buddhist To Practice Buddhism!

Thanks for reading this book! I hope that it's been a useful crash course for you in this swirling world of Eastern religions.

If there's one takeaway, it's that Buddhism is a *forgiving* belief system. Most don't even call it a religion, because there are no gods involved: just a man who decided he would try to show people the path to a good life, and others who believed him for centuries after.

Our Western biblical religions—Christianity, Judaism and Islam—they each evoke a strict adherence to a singular deity, and enforce a stern set of rules on what God allows, what he does not allow and how you will be punished. Each tries to teach morality, good manners and piety—yet each is less through direct supervision and more through stories. The Book of Job does not explicitly tell us *how* to act; rather it tells the story of a man who was punished by God for no apparent reason, and invites us to question God's ways, ultimately hoping that we, in the end, continue to have faith in Him.

Buddhism is different. Buddha did not write a sweeping tome of morality tales. He did not write of Adam and Eve, of Noah's Ark, of David and Goliath; he wrote a very straightforward, not metaphysical, not extraterrestrial, not theological guidebook to life.

Buddhism is, in short, a very *present* belief system. It encourages you to think, feel and breathe in the *now*. Don't worry about karma, don't worry about what comes next: just live your life *now*, be a good person *now*, believe in what exists *now*—and the rest will follow in itself.

In that light, it is easy to take from Buddhism what you will. People from various cultures have been doing this for generations already—Nichiren took a specific section of the Supreme Buddha's final texts; Mahayana Buddhists interpreted his teachings differently than the Arahats; Zen Buddhists differ from tantric Buddhists who different from Tibetan Buddhists who differ from Silla Buddhists.

In other words—the whole thing's being changed as it goes along.

So take what you will, but don't feel confined by what the Buddha teaches. It's a bit of a catch-22: if you aim to achieve nirvana, you'll never achieve it. Only once you stop taking things so seriously, like Bodai the big-bellied laughing Buddha from 10th-century China, and start laughing at things more freely, might you achieve something resembling inner peace.

They're easy words to band about: peace, tranquility, meditation, mindfulness. Calmness. Happiness.

Easier said than done?

I don't think so.

Take up yoga. Buy a plane ticket to India. Start meditating. Listen to the sounds of your breathing. Rub a Bodai's belly for good luck. See where it takes you. Try something new, and try it positively; the worst that can happen is you decide it isn't for you.

So good luck, and remember the old Buddhist saying: "If anything is worth doing, do it with all your heart."

Preview Of "Reiki For Beginners - The Ultimate Guide To Supercharge Your Mind, Increase Your Energy & Feel Great By Unlocking the Power of Reiki"

Chapter 1
What Is All The Fuss About Reiki?

Reiki was developed in the 1880's by a Japanese Buddhist called Dr. Mikao Usui. Reiki means 'spiritually guided life force energy', it is a spiritual energy practice that helps reduce and ease stress and allows the person being healed and treated the energy of complete relaxation in a natural and safe manner.

By helping the body relax you allow the body to re-activate the body's natural healing energy. The techniques used tend to be hands on healing or palm healing and can treat the entire body from emotions, spirit, relaxation, security and wellbeing; this is also known as a method of oriental medicine and a form of self healing.

Dr. Mikao Usui started this healing tradition to ensure that people could be healed by professionals and also be healed by themselves. He would only teach and work with those who truly wished to be healed and would allow their souls to follow the Reiki principles.

The Reiki principles are seen as a valuable tool and technique when practicing Reiki; it allows the patients to become compassionate, generous and to be fully relaxed.

The Reiki Principles:

Just for today, I will not be angry.

Letting go of anger, brings peace into the mind. Anger blocks ones energy, it is an inner enemy.

Just for today, I will not worry.

Letting go of worry, brings healing into the body. Endless worry may hurt ones soul; therefore treatment is required throughout the entire body.

Just for today, I will be grateful.

Being thankful brings joy into the spirit. Simple things such as thanks, smiles and good words can make people happy.

Just for today, I will do my work honestly.

Working honestly brings abundance into the soul. Supporting your family will help you live a respectable life.

Just for today, I will be kind to every living thing.

Being kind brings love into the world. Appreciate your family, friends and elders.

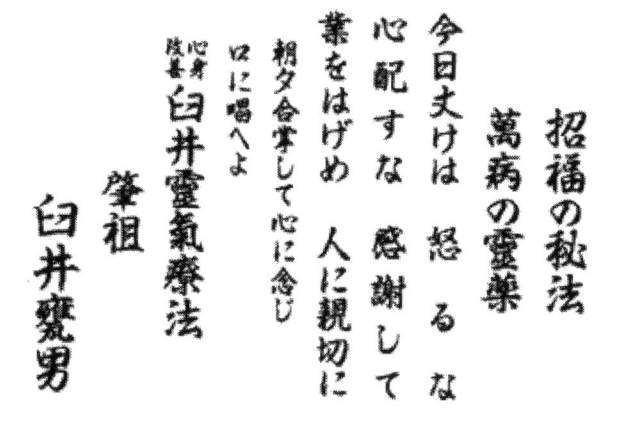

招福の秘法
萬病の靈薬
今日丈けは 怒るな 心配すな 感謝して 業をはげめ 人に親切に
朝夕合掌して心に念じ口に唱へよ
心身改善 臼井靈氣療法
肇祖 臼井甕男

Dr. Usui passed away on 1930 and is know buried in Kyoto temple, the story of this life is written on this gravestone. It is believed that Dr Usui, taught and shared his Reiki techniques with eighteen masters before he died in 1930, one of these masters was called Dr. Chijiro Hayashi.

Dr. Hayashi became the second in line to Dr. Usui and opened a Reiki Clinic in Tokyo, his clinic both taught and healed patients and practioners. Dr Hayashi died on 10th May 1941.

Another master of Dr. Usui was Mrs. Hawayo Takata; she is recognized to have brought Reiki into the western world. She was taught by Dr. Hayashi, she was born in 1900, in Hawaii and treated many patients in the USA. It is believed that she trained up to 20 masters before she passed on 11th December 1980.

The Three Degrees of Reiki

There are three degrees of Reiki; ranging from healing and teaching one on one in the same room to distant teaching around the world.

The First Level

This is called proximity modality healing, the healers has to be near a patient physically to be able to heal them. This involves physical cleansing and can heal discomforts such as the common cold. This level of Reiki can be achieved in one day and is often used to improve the immune system and generally bust the health of those willing.

The Second Level

This is the next step up, it allows the healer to not only heal but teach Reiki across time and space. This means that the healing of Reiki can not only be sent around the world but it can also be sent into the future (time). According to healers in Reiki, time and space do not affect and limit the healing powers of Reiki.

This stage of Reiki is a lot more powerful then degree one, it is advised that the first level of Reiki is practiced for 3 months before level two is considered as it is a lot stronger and can bring back memories from the past and unresolved emotional issues that need to be healed.

The Third Level

This is split into three sections; the Master Healer, the Master (teacher) and the Grandmaster. If you are known as a Master healer you have achieved the highest level of Reiki healing. At this level of Reiki, the healing process can be sent just by thought so therefore the second stage of Reiki should be experienced for 1-3 years to allow the body to get used to the healing process. Positive thinking is essential for this level of practice.

A Master has the ability to teach Reiki to others but only levels one and two whereas the Grandmaster can teach Reiki at all levels.

Chapter 2
Traditional and Western Reiki – The differences!

Traditional Reiki

Dr. Usui

Traditional Reiki is the method that Dr. Usui practiced by after a life a meditation, Buddhism and martial arts. The main goal of traditional Reiki is enlightenment and to be able to achieve a balanced life; he lived by the saying; *'If you can't heal yourself, how can you heal others'*.

The traditional Reiki methods focus on the principles and the use of meditation. The meditation is provided by breathing techniques which help direct the treatment directly to the area that needs healing.

Traditional Reiki is a way of challenging energy through your hands to restore health and well-being, the patient tends to be laid down on a treatment table and the practitioners hands stay still until they need to move the flow of energy through the body.

Western Reiki

Mrs. Hawayo Takata

This is the most common practice of Reiki and is focused mainly on the hands on healing component of Reiki. Not only is it focused on the hands on approach to healing it also includes the healing process known as 'Chakras'.

Chakras

Chakra is connected to the organs in our bodies and the different layer in aura. The word Chakra means 'wheel'; it is a wheel that spins on its own axis in relation to the energy levels in your body. The human body consists of many chakras bodily functions such as breathing, sensory, digestion, secretion, reproduction and circulation.

In total there are seven chakras points which can be focused on to help heal ourselves; the top the head, forehead (also known as the third eye), throat, heart, solar plexus, the navel and the bottom of the pelvis.

This picture shows the positions which can be focused on during Reiki healing through Chakras.

The top of the head (also known as the crown)

Identity, self knowledge and thought are all aspects of the crown element.

This does not just focus on the mind it is related to the whole body, the entire being. Once this chakras is developed it brings the patient wisdom, knowledge, understanding and bliss. It is the connection to the great world and our consciousness.

The third eye

Self reflection, light and identity are all aspects of the third eye element.

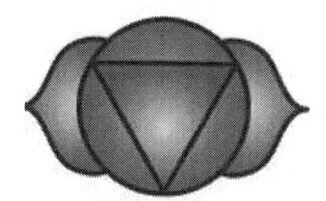

This belongs to the brain and facial features such as the eyes, nose and mouth. When this area is healed it allows us to 'see the bigger picture', to see clearly and get a better understanding of ourselves.

The throat

The aspects of this element are self reflection, creative identity and light.

This corresponds to the patient's throat and lungs; can be focused on when suffering with breathing problems. Once healed it allows us to have great creativity and communication.

The heart

This element has many aspects from social identity and self acceptance.

This chakra focuses on the heart and the arms. When this chakra is healed it allows us to feel compassion, love deeply and have a sense of peace and harmony.

The solar perplex

The aspects related to this element are self-definition and ego identity.

This covers many areas such as the liver, bladder, stomach, small intestine and the spleen. This is the power chakra, when it is healed and is healthy it brings us energy, personal power and a healthy metabolism.

The navel

Emotional identity and self gratification are both aspects of this element of the Chakras.

This chakra focuses on the reproduction systems, the urinary bladder and kidneys; it tends to be the focus when the patient is suffering from water infections or kidney pains. This is our connection chakras to other people through the feelings of desire and sensation. When healed this element brings us a great depth of feeling, sexual fulfilment and the ability to accept change in others.

The bottom of the pelvis (also known as the root)

The main aspects of this element are self preservation and physical identity.

This includes the large intestine and the rectum and can also help heal the kidneys if needed. As this chakras is located at the bottom of the spine it forms the foundation of our bodies, once healed this chakras should bring health, security and prosperity to the patient.

To check out the rest of *"Reiki For Beginners - The Ultimate Guide To Supercharge Your Mind, Increase Your Energy & Feel Great By Unlocking the Power of Reiki"*, **go to Amazon and look for it right now!**

Ps: You'll find many more books like these under my name, Dominique Francon.
Don't miss them! Here's a short list:

- Buddhism For Beginners
- Meditation For Beginners

- Reiki For Beginners
- Yoga For Beginners

- Running Will Make You FIT
- Cycling HIIT Training

- Paleo Recipe Cookbooks
- Much, much more!

About the Author

Dominique Francon is a significant health connoisseur devoted to helping others get healthy all around the world.

From a very young age, Francon understood the value and potential of leading a healthy lifestyle. And because of her genuine appreciation and enthusiasm for all things health-related, she has dedicated a great deal of time and effort to researching the best of what fitness, nutritional diets and overall wellbeing programs have to offer.

In the beginning, Francon focused on working with people in various gym and sports club settings. Before long she became exceedingly in tune with the health and fitness solutions that had the best results for her clients' issues and goals. But after years of accumulating one health expertise following another, Francon decided she wanted to reach out to even more individuals.

She wanted to help people on a bigger scale. For this reason she resolved to share her extensive knowledge with people through writing and publishing books pertaining to her vast health-related know-how. Currently she has authored books on such cutting-edge topics as paleo cooking, Zen, Yoga, running and cycling.

Francon has a real passion for all the subjects she writes about and she takes the job seriously. She knows self-development is, for a lot of people, as significant as it is for her. But she also knows how tough it is to change one's lifestyle. With this in mind, her aim while writing is to make the concepts and instructions as helpful and accessible to her readers as possible. After all, for her the end objective is improving the lives of others.

Printed in Great Britain
by Amazon.co.uk, Ltd.,
Marston Gate.